CARMEN LECCARDI, PAOLO JEDLOWSKI
AND ALESSANDRO CAVALLI

EXPLORING NEW TEMPORAL HORIZONS

A Conversation between Memories and Futures

BRISTOL
UNIVERSITY
PRESS

First published in Great Britain in 2023 by

Bristol University Press
University of Bristol
1–9 Old Park Hill
Bristol
BS2 8BB
UK
t: +44 (0)117 374 6645
e: bup-info@bristol.ac.uk

Details of international sales and distribution partners are available at bristoluniversitypress.co.uk

British Library Cataloguing in Publication Data
A catalogue record for this book is available from the British Library

ISBN 978-1-5292-1397-3 hardcover
ISBN 978-1-5292-1398-0 ePub
ISBN 978-1-5292-1399-7 ePdf

Cover design: blu inc
Front cover image: Antonio Pio Roseti
(instagram.com/antoniopioroseti)

Contents

Introduction

The key idea behind this book can be summarized as follows: the study of temporal perspectives and the changes brought about by historical processes can help the social sciences recompose what other disciplines have gradually separated and fragmented, and oftentimes contrasted. In a global society full of conflicts that have only been partially analysed, we need a global approach. A temporal analysis can both sustain this approach and concretely express it. Using time as an analytic tool, the defence of life in the Anthropocene and the fight against unacceptable levels of economic and social inequality – not only between the Global North and South but also within individual societies – can become part of the same global justice project.

In this framework, we first need to identify the signals coming from free civil society and amplify its call for a radical change of direction. Depending on the possibilities available to us today, we must redefine our horizons with regard to both the climate crisis and the 'reasonable utopias' that promote respect for the moral ideal of equality. We can therefore affirm that while focusing on a redefinition of the concepts of memory and future in the first decades of the new century, and exploring how the very concept of generation has been transformed in this context, this book advances a distinctly political perspective.

The book's title refers to the theme of temporal horizons (Husserl, 1964 [1928]), which, for many decades, have been affected by a process of contraction or shrinkage that has challenged some of the axioms of modernity (Di Chio, 2015). This choice was the result of a precise analytical itinerary. Given the effect of the 'closure of time' on the present, which damages its essential relationship with the past and the medium- to long-term future, this process impacts the very life of institutions and social groups, as well as the lives of single individuals. The forms and exercise of democracy, collective action, symbolic and communicative expressions, biographical constructions and identities, social reproduction and conflict, the relationships among generations, and even – and most importantly – the concept of action itself are profoundly changed by this deep transformation. At the core of this change, which the book explores through the lens of its own temporal code (for example, a reflection on the past and memory, on the future and future projects, and on generations), is a constellation of elements, as Hartmut Rosa (2010, 2013) aptly highlighted in his analyses of high-speed society. These include the structural needs of contemporary capitalism, which can be defined as the need for 'dynamic stabilization' (Torres and Rosa, 2021: 520). This stabilization can apparently only be safeguarded through further forms of acceleration, especially the increasingly extreme technological ones.

These general observations suggest that we approach time in a Durkheimian way as a veritable social institution. Thus, time represents an ordering principle, tied to the coordination and normative character of social life. However, time also provides the basis for the sheer expression of agency (Adam, 1995). For instance, the social movements involved in climate activism, which are currently fighting against the 'end of time' that they believe will accompany the most nefarious outcome of the contemporary climate crisis, are a direct expression of this. Moreover, considering biographical narrations, the concept of 'time work' (Flaherty, 2013) – which re-elaborates agency in a temporal key, building forms of memory and projects that can give personal gratification – shows that time can become an instrument of self-determination and freedom for the individual. Recent research on the use of 'time work' among younger generations has stressed this tendency (Leccardi, 2021). Ultimately, when it comes to temporal experience, we are faced with a 'complicated mixture of determinism and self-determination' (Flaherty, 2020: 14; see also Cuzzocrea and Mandich, 2015; Cook, 2018).

Returning to what we have called the book's 'political framework', and before taking a closer look at its structure and contents, we need to make a few more considerations that will explain why we have chosen temporal horizons and their contraction as the unifying theme of the book. First of all, we are currently faced with the diffusion – in both public opinion and collective consciousness – of a feeling of powerlessness and disaffiliation with regard to processes of social and political change that are accelerating and, at least apparently, chaotic. It is therefore imperative, even for sociological research, to go back to the 'perspective of the possible' (Guégen and Laurent, 2022), that is, the need to adopt a perspective that sees not only limitations but also possibilities in the present. From this viewpoint, the possible is now being shaped by new kinds of utopias. A good example is the 'ecological utopia' embodied by the environmentalist movements, which is analysed throughout the book, as it represents the possibility of reversing the race to destroy the planet and the life it harbours based on a commitment to the here and now. According to the scientific world, this race is bound to intensify as the months go by, and the climate crisis we are experiencing is a direct indicator of this process. In this regard, it is worth recalling the thoughts Max Weber expressed in his 1917 methodological essay 'Der Sinn der "Wertfreiheit" der soziologischen und őkonomischen Wissenschaften' (see Weber, 2012). Here, Weber reminds us that successful politics always results from the application of some form of 'art of the impossible' and, particularly, that success is achieved 'only because the impossible was sought' in the pursuit of the objective.

Second, we are convinced that the social sciences can contribute to the understanding of new codes of communication and the construction of meaning in a global society where information has become a fundamental resource

(Melucci, 1996). In our opinion, the study of temporal dynamics can greatly facilitate this understanding.

***

The horizon – that line that confuses Heaven and Earth, opening up a broad and intangible perspective, and simultaneously delimiting space – is at the centre of the relationship between what is determined and what is not. The horizon easily draws attention to the ambivalences of human experience. The metaphor of the horizon as a direction towards which to strive – potentially with a utopian function – can also be useful in social and temporal reflection. As others have written (Di Chio, 2015: 19, our translation), just as a human being on an island 'can control, evaluate and face only that portion of the sea that is defined by the horizon, so a society remembers, admires and plans based on this moving boundary'.

As a social construction, the time horizon therefore plays a powerful, albeit concealed, role in constructing what we could call the 'cultural environment' of an era. If modernity – when it was at its height – expanded temporal horizons, propelled by the powerful ideology of progress, combining optimism and rationality in the belief that it could consider the future an open and susceptible time *a-venir* (one of the current French translations of future), things are now different. We have already discussed this and would rather like to emphasize the relationship between this conceptual construction and the articulation of the book. For example, if we want to reflect on temporal horizons, why dwell not only on the future but also on the past (through memory) and the theme of generations?

In social phenomenology, 'the world in actual reach has essentially the temporal character of the present' (Schutz and Luckmann, 1973: 51). The present is, then, the locus of action. Yet, in this representation, the present is not an isolated temporal instance; on the contrary, it is closely connected to the past and the future. The three levels seem so intertwined and inseparable as to prevent any considerations and analyses that lack continuous references to one another. After all, did Husserl (1964 [1928]) not say that through protention and retention, the open and porous present is constantly infiltrated by temporal perspectives linked to the past and the future? By focusing on action, social phenomenology seeks to accentuate this analytical tendency. From this viewpoint, action is not only always directed to the future but also integrated into time by references to the past. Memory filters the past and prepares it to connect to the future through a process within which the available knowledge (the 'stock of knowledge', or '*Wissensvorrat*', in Schutz's words) plays a strategic role.

Nevertheless, the phenomenological approach – as much as, for example, Mead's (1954 [1932]) view, even though from a different analytical perspective – rejects any form of determinism. Whether it is the past's influence on the present or the future's symmetrical imprint on the present, this analytical perspective mainly seeks to highlight the nexus between freedom, the 'emergence of the new' and the 'creativity of action' (Joas, 1996).

The limited space of this introduction does not allow to discuss the complex Schutzian construction of the interweaving of action, time and the life-world (see Adam, 1990: esp 34ff). Instead, we wish to highlight the conceptual junctures that have had the greatest influence on the book's general itinerary.

Chapter One, 'Memories: What Memories Does the Future Need?', adheres to this non-deterministic perspective. It reminds us that memories are selective and constitute an interpretation and reconstruction of past events in the light of present interests and priorities, on the one hand, and future expectations, on the other (Jedlowski and Pellegrino, 2020). The basic question that guides the chapter (What memories does the future need?) finds a plurality of answers in the presented analytical articulation. Within these answers, though, the key point is that of the circularity between past and future. Thanks to this feature, subjects and groups can work through even extremely painful pasts, including traumatic ones. However, the chapter claims that it is often necessary to also deal with past times of hopes that have not been fulfilled – past futures, or memories concerning once-imagined futures. Nowadays, the increasing fragmentation and multiplication of views on the past produced by new media, in particular, along with the exponential growth of what can potentially be preserved, complicates the work of memory and, additionally, its close relationship with forms of experience. Within a contracted time horizon, deprived of desirable futures, memories can multiply by presenting themselves as a refuge from a social time that is experienced as a threat.

Chapter Two is titled 'Futurity: Changing Futures in a Changing World' and is not only traversed but structured – directly or indirectly – by a reflection on the nexus between past, present and future. In the construction of Western modernity, as early as the 17th century, the representation of the future as a time full of potential to be enthusiastically explored played a primary role. This process ran parallel to the devaluation of the past, considered cumbersome and worthless. Detached from all predetermination and restored to human history, the future proudly disengaged itself from references to the past. The ideology of progress reinforced this *zeitgeist*; it focused on the present and tied it inextricably to conquest and domination, including colonial domination. The chapter reconstructs the different stages of this process up to the present day. After two world wars, the Bomb and the Shoah, the future is no longer a time of enchantment. Quite the contrary: it usually only arouses fear, and people try to bypass it in the most suitable ways, for example, by focusing on the present. The massive acceleration of social life, perhaps even more so in the new millennium, has, in turn, increased a widespread sense of insecurity and the uncontrollability of personal and social changes. According to the global climate movement, this feeling can and must be transformed into an urgent and generalized demand for 'alternative futures' (Pleyers, 2020).

The dramatic war that has been on Europe's doorstep since February 2022, following the Russian invasion of Ukraine, underscores the rationality of this demand.

Chapter Three, 'Memory and Future through the Generations', deals with a classic theme in sociology: time and generations. The chapter picks up the issue of the circularity between past and future from the perspective of generations, the de facto mediators between the collective and individual dimensions of time. In addition to unprecedented structural aspects (starting with multigenerational societies where – in the Global North – the older generations tend to prevail in number, thus exercising direct forms of control over available resources), it also highlights the existence of new areas of conflict. As both the outcome of processes of socio-historical change and the origin of social and political transformation, generations emerge as a social entity at the boundary between history and memory. At present, though, the contraction of temporal horizons is calling into question the collective identities that they have traditionally borne, as the chapter emphasizes. In the increasingly present-focused environment that is thus created, the past and the future wear away; memories and projects can, in turn, become disconnected, producing types of 'generational consciousness' in which individualization becomes an essential reference point. Yet, the recent emergencies created by the COVID-19 pandemic, on the one hand, and the climate crisis, on the other, have opened up the possibility of new forms of intergenerational solidarity. The 'European war' provoked by the Russian invasion of Ukraine increases this need. Focusing on the climate crisis, one aspect stands out: since the responsibility for the current global environmental disaster lies with the older generations, they must assume it publicly. Only thus can a new pact between the generations be built.

ONE

Memories: What Memories Does the Future Need?

Memento

As teachers, we often discuss the topic of memory with our students, and sometimes they protest: 'Why do we have to talk about the past? It's the future we care about!' But are they really two separate things? During a lecture, we were once rescued by a story told by a friend of ours. It is a story taken from daily life.

Our friend lives in Rome, a crowded city. Every night, when he drives home, he has to circle his neighbourhood many times to find a parking spot. He is rather forgetful, and he knows that. Finding his car the next morning is often a problem. The solution he has found is that every night, when he gets home, he tells his wife where he parked: "Saying it out loud is really helpful, you know", he said, "Then we both know where the car is."

In this story, especially in our friend's comment, there is something that is relevant to our discussion of memory, which is that memory has a power to 'exteriorize' itself. Saying out loud to another person where we parked the car is a form of exteriorization of personal memory, that is, of the human capacity to store a memory outside of ourselves. We might as well say that memory has a power to 'objectivize' itself: if our friend was more familiar with his smartphone, he could save the spot in a note or take a picture of the street, or he might, more simply, write it on a piece of paper.

This is the method used by the protagonist of Christopher Nolan's (2000) film *Memento* to exteriorize his memory. This character suffers from anterograde amnesia, a disorder that makes him able to retain whatever happens to him only for a few minutes before it fades away. His life is a series of unrelated episodes with no memory to tie them together – which clearly makes it a very hard life. We might take this disorder as a metaphor of modern life, that is, of the disconnected character of our experiences in the frantic rhythm of the daily grind. To alleviate the effects of his disorder, this character has learned to leave written notes to himself: he writes them on pieces of paper and on the bathroom mirror, and even gets the most important things tattooed on his own skin. In this way, through each of the disjointed episodes that make up his life, he preserves what he thinks he will need in the future to avoid having to start from scratch each time.

The story of our friend and his parking spots has something quite similar to it because the underlying problem is the same: preserving some traces of the past in order to orient oneself in the future. More generally, this is the logic behind every learning: if we retain what we have learned, whether consciously or unconsciously, it is because we think we might use it in the future. Those who forget their mistakes are bound to repeat them.

No doubt, this service performed by memory for the future harbours a risk: what we learn can turn into a propensity to look at novelty through our learned lens. Obviously, this may not be functional. However, letting our thoughts and our actions become immobilized by the past is a pathological way of using memory: while there is some degree of inertia to learned thoughts and behaviours, the interplay between established knowledge and openness to novelty is generally dynamic in adequately healthy people. In fact, we can only start from what we learned, but then we challenge it, thus renewing the learning experience (Gadamer, 2013).

By this point, our students are usually interested but still sceptical: if too much change occurs, past knowledge only has limited value. Indeed, our modern world is in rapid and constant change, and we will discuss this. Before such a discussion, however, we must note at least one of the other common ways in which memory and future are intertwined: one of those phenomena psychologists define as 'prospective memory' – a difficult expression to describe very simple facts. For instance, when we look at our planner (whether physical or digital), what does it contain? Written signs to remind us of our appointments, which can be a lecture, a doctor appointment or a mortgage payment that needs to be made. They are things 'to do', that is, that will happen in the future. However, we took note of them in the past; hence, they reside in our memory. This is what we call 'prospective memory'. This is a form of memory we use all the time. Without it, our social life would be impossible.

Here, again, we find the same idea suggested by our friend's story: memory has a service relationship with the future. It should be noted, however, that the invitation to remember something that will happen in the future was also implied in the title of the film we quoted earlier: *Memento* (Nolan, 2000). 'Memento' is a Latin word, a verb in the imperative form: it means 'Remember!' It is an invitation we find – explicit or implicit – on tombstones, on monuments and in ceremonies: intentions of memory and invitations to the future at the same time. Here, memory shows another of its basic functions: the things that ask to be remembered are very often warnings. 'Remember to …' – we say it often, to every child, to every husband who forgets to close the door behind him and to every lover when we leave: 'remember me'.

There is, perhaps, something of a moral warning in the notes we write to track our appointments: forgetting an event or a deadline to which we had committed ourselves is socially reproachable. However, the invitation to remember may indeed have a larger, or deeper, link with morality. This is just a vague hint (we have no time to develop this point now), but we must mention it: 'remember' is one of the key words of the Bible – *Zakhor*.

Zakhor is the Jewish word for 'Remember!' The Jews saying this word to themselves were referring to past vicissitudes (the exile or the exodus) as much as to a future: what had to be kept in mind was the covenant tying them to their God, a promise. What needed to be remembered were a past and a future, *together*. It was an invitation to 'keep in mind' – this might be the expression in which the relation between memory and future is most apparent. Let us keep that in mind as well; it might prove useful.

Individual and collective memories

To discuss these issues, we need to consider the evidence provided by memory studies, as well as by future studies. In this chapter, we will focus on the former's perspective.

Memory studies are a bustling interdisciplinary galaxy. This book does not aim to provide an overview of them (on this, see Tota and Hagen, 2016), but we can point at their most important traits, especially those that will be most useful in highlighting the links between memories and representations of the future.

The first of these links can be expressed in several ways, but the simplest way is the one used by Henri Bergson (1988 [1896]) in the early days of 20th-century studies on this topic: the distinction between *mémoire-image* and *mèmoire-habitude*. The former includes mental representations of the past, what we generally call actual 'memories'; the latter comprises the knowledge we incorporated in the past, which is extended in the form of capacities and active dispositions in the present.

When we talk about memory in everyday language, we usually refer to *mémoire-image*: the images of the past that are available to us. This is what we will mostly cover in this book.

However, the second form is equally important and must be mentioned, even if we will only marginally touch on it. Without the memories we progressively incorporate, life would be impossible – and these are nothing like what we usually call memories. Consider the act of driving a car: the fact that we 'remember' how to do it does not mean we remember when we learned, the face of the instructor or our first mistakes. We are activating knowledge that we acquired in the past but has become part of our present: a behaviour scheme, or a skill.

Even in collective life, there is something akin to a *mémoire-habitude*. As we will see, collective memory can be intended as the ensemble of images of the past maintained by a group. However, groups also remember in other ways: through traditions, institutions and routines. Each in its own way, these realms incorporate, so to speak, some pasts and transmit them by anticipating part of what lies ahead for the group members. They fix what has been learned in systems of rules, norms, behaviour schemes and expectation frameworks, which, unless major changes occur, remain part of our living present. It is true that modern culture has drastically reduced the legitimizing power of traditions, making institutions increasingly unstable, and has often expressed a genuine dislike of routines. However, without routines, daily life would be impossible. Despite the focus on the present that seems to characterize the lives of individuals and groups today, some degree of social *mémoire-habitude* survives.

However, as we said, we will mainly talk about *mémoire-image* – the memories we keep of something that happened in the past. In light of everything we know today, the metaphor of memory as an 'inventory' no longer holds: memory is a set of functions in which the past is much more movable than we would like to think. The past leaves tracks, but it is the present that selects these tracks on each occasion, interpreting them and reconstructing them.

Mnestic processes are *selective*: the choice of what is retained from the past is dictated by the present and its interests. Mnestic processes are *interpretative*: the present not only selects certain elements of the past but also interprets them, giving them a specific meaning, attaching feelings to them and judging them. Ultimately, mnestic processes are *constructive*: representations of the past are mediated by symbolic frameworks, primarily by those implicit in language itself.

These thoughts were formulated during the first half of the 20th-century by such authors as Maurice Halbwachs, George Herbert Mead, Frederic Barlett and Pierre Janet. Later research has been more sophisticated but has confirmed their validity. Among the authors we cited, Maurice Halbwachs (1925, 1997 [1950], 2008 [1941]) was undoubtedly the most influential. It is primarily to him that we owe the formulation of the most important element of memory studies as a whole: the idea that it is difficult, if not impossible, to be completely alone in remembering.

Concretely, and based on an impressive body of research, we can say that the discourses on the past happening around us set the degree of plausibility of individual memories: if our recalling of the past is inconsistent with the versions supported by others, it becomes difficult even for us to be certain. Furthermore, where plausibility is not contested, the relevance of what we remember is still subjected to the collective discourse: what no one around us confirms or mentions tends to fade from our discourses on the past and, at least in part, from our own memory, as if it were ultimately irrelevant.

Individual memories, then, have a tight relationship with what we could call *collective memories*. This expression, originally proposed by Halbwachs, is not without its ambiguities and has been the object of much discussion (Olick et al, 2011). We might define collective memory as 'a set of social representations concerning the past which each group produces, institutionalizes, guards and transmits through the interaction of its members' (Jedlowski, 2001: 33). The origin and basic mechanisms of the construction and reconstruction of collective memory operate at the level of the communication practices embedded in daily life (Namer, 1987). However, these practices can solidify in rituals, commemorations, monuments and so on, thus becoming reference points of the individual memory of each one of us.

A subset of collective memory is what could be called 'historic memory'. This is a relatively less-used expression across memory studies. Indeed, there is some ambiguity to it because it unites two opposing terms: 'history', as the object of historiography, seeks the ascertainment of what should be, at least ideally, the objective truth. It relies on the rigorous use of sources, the formulation of hypotheses and the repeated assessment of their plausibility by a scientific community. 'Memory', on the contrary, is subjective, has an immediate utility for life, is relatively unconcerned with verifying its contents and is often careless about the deformations it applies to the past. Nevertheless, the expression 'historical memory' is a useful one: it alludes to representations of events, people, situations or objects that an individual did not necessarily experience directly but belong to a collective past that has accompanied or preceded their life, so that they possess a memory of them, which is largely mediated by other people's reports. The function of historical memory is to situate subjects in history – not as a knowledge of it but as a lived connection.

The objectivization of historical memories in modern times has been a constant effort of national states, which took it upon themselves to embody them in monuments, tombs, commemorations and speeches, and to promote their interiorization through their education systems. Primarily, these have been celebrative memories, such as of foundational events and national glories, being useful in legitimizing identity and missions. This helps compensate for internal differences related to class, income, regional cultures and sometimes ethnicity by referring to an identity whose basis is essentially territorial and defined by land borders. However, the stability of borders and populations do not stay reliable for very long (Connerton, 2009). Throughout the 1900s, European borders have changed over and over; migrations, forced transfers, deportations and mobility of all sorts have severed the links between memories and territories, and between collective memories and feelings of belonging. Moreover, the complexity of modern societies makes it increasingly difficult to identify belonging. For Halbwachs, who lived in the golden age of nation states, the primary function of collective memory was to facilitate the cohesion of societies by granting them a particular identity. However, in the modern world, identities cannot be taken for granted; rather, multiple historical memories are formed, and a 'national' collective memory is hard (though not entirely impossible) to forge. What is left, then, is a battlefield.

The construction of a collective memory is always a process that implies conflict, negotiations and compromise. However, if multiple collective memories are at play, the conflict dimension tends to take centre stage. If one group has a preponderance of power, censorship can happen and rival versions can be banned. More often, certain representations of the past become 'hegemonic': they manage to impose themselves, becoming a sort of historical common sense within a given population. They assert themselves not by force but through daily communication practices.

The relationship between collective memories and power may be the topic that memory studies have covered the most. For our book's theme, we must note that this relationship also implies a link between representations of the past and of the future. When power takes interest in a past, it does so primarily to legitimize a project, as shown by the famous George Orwell quote: 'Who controls the past controls the future' (Orwell, 1949: 44). The elites use historical memory to build a tradition to which they declare themselves the heirs and that, while legitimizing them, also supports their projects for the future – a future that is presented as the completion of that tradition. In Orwell's novel, this construction was completely arbitrary, but in reality, the elements that make up these historical memories are usually based on historically proven facts that were often spontaneously preserved by collective memory. These, however, are carefully selected, interpreted and recreated to be consistent with present interests, while incongruous elements are removed.

Spaces of experience and horizons of expectations

So far, we have seen how it can be useful to preserve some traces of the past and that it can be done intentionally (as powers, but also individuals, do). However, the past matters even when we do not remember it. The conditions of the present have been laid out in the past: they are its result; they depend upon it. The present, we might say, is not born in the present. Nor does the future originate in the future; rather, it is a continuation, a development or an unfolding of something that is contained in the present as a potential. There are ongoing tendencies in the present, probably many of them at all times. These tendencies can be at odds with each other, and different groups can be trying to advance some of them, so that the actual future will never be the mere unfolding of a single tendency but a tangle of them. Either way, the future will be a product of the present.

What concerns us in this book, however, is not the future in itself but the relationship between memory and what we imagine regarding the future. The past is always more than what we consciously recall, and the possible future is always wider than what we can imagine. With that said, what can memory teach us, today, about imagining the future? Not much at all, said Reinhart Koselleck (1985) in his *Futures Past*. This is an important book, whose central theme is the relationship between what Koselleck calls the 'space of experience' and the 'horizon of expectations' – a relationship that, according to him, is in crisis in the modern age. Let us explain this relationship before commenting on it.

Koselleck (1985: 272) defines experience as 'present past, whose events have been incorporated and can be remembered'. It is individual but always contains and preserves 'an element of alien experience conveyed by generations or institutions' (Koselleck, 1985: 272). Expectation is similar in many ways: expectation also takes place in the today; it is the future made present. Like experience, it is at once person specific and interpersonal. However, the presence of the past is different than that of the future: the legibility of the future confronts an absolute limit, for it cannot be experienced.

In pre-modern worlds, the space of past experiences and the horizons of expectations about the future had a tight relationship; in fact, they were united. In an essentially stable world, what could be expected was prefigured by what had already been experienced in the past. However, this relationship enters a crisis in modern times. As Koselleck (1985: 276) put it: 'During *Neuzeit* the difference between experience and expectation has increasingly expanded; more precisely … *Neuzeit* is first understood as a *neue Zeit* [new time] from the time that expectations have distanced themselves evermore from all previous experience.'

The space of experience and the horizons of expectations tend to disassociate in modern times. It is hard to deny it. By its very essence, modernity is the age of novelty; it is constant change. Not accidental change, which had always been known, but, rather, change as the rule. As Charles Baudelaire (2010 [1863]: 13) wrote: modernity is the age of 'the transient, the fleeting, the contingent'.

Baudelaire also said that cities transform more rapidly than the heart of men, but this was not always the case. In a pre-modern society, or in a pre-industrial world, a man could reasonably expect that his town and the places where he lived would not change during his lifetime, unless extraordinary events occurred. Baudelaire's quote only acquires its meaning when compared with the modern environment. It is here that, for the first time, and on a mass scale, rethinking our past lives means, for each of us, seeing changes that impacted not only ourselves – coming of age or the vicissitudes of our biography – but also the entire world surrounding us. Indeed, so great is the speed of change in the world around us that the individual appears still by comparison: stuck on the things they learned to love, they see the world in which their existence took shape shattered into pieces. This is the reason why modern humans know so intimately the theme of 'lost time'.

However, things are more complex than this: when Baudelaire wrote that modernity is the transient, the fugitive and the contingent, in the following line, he added that this is only a half of it, the other being the eternal and the immovable. Underlying change, according to Baudelaire, there is something permanent. Baudelaire talked as a poet – we will not attempt to define eternity. However, his sentence, as vague as it may be, calls on us: there is something unchanging, it says, about human experience.

Indeed, there are aspects of our nature that have persisted since the birth of homo sapiens neume. Motives of action, passions and feelings acquire different cultural frameworks throughout history, but if we can read Homer, it is because we recognize something in it. Sure, the theme of human nature is a complex one, and this is not the time to tackle it. However, we can at least remind ourselves that change always has multiple rhythms. Every psychologist knows that the times of material life and those of psychic life are different. However, even in the social world, not everything changes at the same time or at the same speed in different areas of the planet, in different groups of a society, in different areas of life or even within the same person.

Partly for such reasons as these, historians have proposed the idea of 'long duration'. The *longue dureé* was the keyword of the '*nouvelle histoire*' of Fernand Braudel and his colleagues of the review *Annales*. What Braudel means is that beneath the history of events, there is a longer and slower history, in which things change at a different pace, and even when they change, they do so slowly and following deeper revolutions than the ones a historian interested only in 'events' can see. In particular, the means of production, they noted, change more slowly and for different reasons than political structures, while the same technologies that change so rapidly today were virtually unchanged for millennia. We might add that religious belief too changes according to different rhythms, as well as the mythical patrimonies that provide the basis for tales. The list could go on and on and would make for an interesting exploration. Koselleck himself admitted as much. In his following writings, he recognized that his diagnosis only applies to certain areas of our experience: it is clear that there are long-term structures that are preserved through human history without being affected by technical-industrial progress.

What elaborating the past means

The divarication of the 'space of experiences' and the 'horizon of expectations', then, is a partial diagnosis. It would not be appropriate to conclude that the past, for us, is silent.

To complete our discourse, we need to challenge the concept of 'experience'. In *Futures Past*, Koselleck (1985) defines experience as everything we have learned throughout our life: it is the result of learnings whose function is ultimately adaptive, which evidently means that changes in the environment can make unsuitable what used to be suitable. However, the word 'experience' also has other meanings. It can be meant as the result of reflection. In order to have experience of something, living it is not enough; rather, it often needs to be relived to disclose its meaning.

What makes it challenging to relive our experience in this sense is the speed at which we live today. This is the conclusion of Hartmut Rosa's (2010) book *Alienation and Acceleration*: living in a rush, we lack time to reflect; we live many experiences, but we do not have experience anymore. We alienate ourselves, he argues, from our own lives. Thus, the issue is not change in itself but the rush, the speed, the acceleration.

Experience entails not only what we have lived but also what we are able to say about it, what we understood of it and the meaning we attach to it. In this sense, experience eludes Koselleck's diagnosis because change itself does not destroy it; rather, it depends on it.

The past can leave us with questions that, when they are left unanswered, do not result in a freer future. Quite the opposite: the past, unless it is turned into experience, can hold us hostage.

To understand this point, it is useful to recall, as an example, the history of Holocaust memory. This history unfolded in several phases. The period before 1960 is known as the years of silence; this phase was followed by the years of the return of the repressed, then by the age of testimonies and, finally, by what could be called a phase of consolidation and articulation of the issue. These phases have affected all the areas of European public life. This journey has made the Holocaust, today, the centre of some kind of 'civic religion' in Europe, a religion based on the invitation to *not forget* what we want to never happen again.

What this means in regard to our topic is that if there was a traumatic experience, in order to recognize the trauma, we need to talk about it: memories need to be spoken (Alexander et al, 2004). Memory, in this case, does not immediately appear useful; rather, it hurts. However, it does serve a purpose, a fundamental one, as if we want to keep something horrible from happening again, we need to remember it. It is the only way to investigate and contrast its causes. Memory serves the future, and in this light, modernity does not supplant it at all; rather, modernity needs memory.

This is what Adorno (1986 [1959]) warmly suggested to the Germans, who were eager to forget, in a radio conference titled 'The Meaning of Working through the Past'. The German title contained a special expression, 'working through', which Adorno took from common parlance and repurposed as a key concept for the discussion of memory.

As a concept, the expression 'working through' comes from the language of psychoanalysis. The term '*Verarbeitung*' was used by Sigmund Freud to refer to specific modes of 'work' that happen partly within the psyche and partly in the relationship between the patient and their analyst. It is a process of reconsideration of experience, whose purpose is similar not only to a recognition or acceptance by the patient of the removed contents but also to the patient's liberation, as a consequence, from the influence of the repetitive mechanisms caused by the fixation of the unresolved trauma in certain symptoms: when trauma that has not been dealt with locks the future in malaise, memory is the only force that can free the future.

Memory, indeed, is more than what we can consciously remember. However, we can question memory and bring to consciousness what we have removed. This is a particular mode of mnestic work: the act of working through replaces the automatic functioning of the mechanisms of erasure, which tend to exclude from consciousness everything problematic or distressing, with a conscious act of confrontation with the negative, with what distresses us, disturbs us and undermines us.

As for Adorno, his merit lies in having first used the term outside the context of psychoanalysis. Later on, its translation to the field of human sciences was completed by other authors, such as Dominick LaCapra (1994) in *Representing the Holocaust* (see also Ricoeur, 2004). In sociology, 'working through' became the name of a process in which a group takes responsibility for its own history (Habermas, 1986).

It is an act of recognition of what was lived, breaking through the censorship imposed by public discourse and by the individuals themselves. This recognition implies an understanding of the very reasons why we censored it. All this pays a service to the future because liberation from trauma is achieved not by simply moving away from the past but, rather, through its acceptance. There are many forms of obliviousness; some are necessary, but the obliviousness of what we are responsible for is not among these (Weinrich, 2004).

Experiences

Working through the past is not exclusively an individual effort. In order to work through the past, we need to be able to recount it. To this end, the legitimacy afforded by public discourses is critical: what the collective does not recognize remains silent.

This is a problem faced by all the pasts that for some reason can be defined as traumatic, painful or controversial. The literature on this topic nowadays is immense (trauma studies, in particular, have almost become an autonomous section of memory studies). However, traumatic pasts are not the only pasts that ask to be worked through. The past always requires revisiting to some degree. Otherwise, we could hardly call it 'experience'. In this respect, a quote from the work of an anthropologist, Victor Turner (1982: 18), is especially useful: 'An experience is incomplete, unless one of its "moments" is "performance", an act of creative retrospection, in which "meaning" is ascribed to the events and parts of the experience – even if the meaning is that "there is no meaning".'

Experience can be incomplete. To understand this point, we need to widen our scope. As we indicated, the word 'experience' has many different meanings. By our definition, its richness lies in the fact that it can point to the totality of what we experience in life as much as to the ability to reconsider what we have lived and assign a meaning to it. In this sense, it is a process. Since we do not exactly know what we are living while we live it, its comprehension is akin to 'thinking back': going back to what we lived while recognizing that we were at first, at least in part, in the dark about it.

Besides Adorno, who we referenced earlier, this thought permeates all the Frankfurt School, especially Walter Benjamin's works. The German word Benjamin used to call experience was '*Erfahrung*', as opposed to '*Erlebnis*', which denotes experience as a punctual event. *Erfahrung* is a process, whether the word is used to describe practical learning arising from repeated practice or a revisitation of the past that enables the subject to attribute meaning to it.

However, for Benjamin (2002 [1936], 2003 [1940]), experience runs the risk of atrophy in the modern age. Full of *Erlebnisse* as we are, we can be *Erfahrung*-poor. This is due to the fragmentation of life into disconnected realms and to the speed of change and the ever-faster rhythms in which each of us is engaged. Benjamin knew Nietzsche: the tempo of modernity is prestissimo. The atrophy of *Erfahrung* is a defence from the excess of stimuli implied by the prestissimo. However, this atrophy also leads to a sort of aphasia because it implies a separation of lived experiences from the possibility of culturally mediated conscious access to their mnestic traces.

In some of Benjamin's works, however, there are elements that mitigate this radical diagnosis. When Benjamin (2002 [1936]: 316) names Proust, he speaks of his writing as an effort 'to restore the figure of the storyteller to the current generation'. However, restoring the figure of the storyteller amounts precisely to restoring the possibility to communicate experience. Proust's work, says Benjamin, gives an idea of the difficulty of this effort in our age, but it also shows a way for it. No doubt, this is a different kind of experience from its traditional counterpart. As suggested by the example of Proust, experience in the modern age is primarily the outcome of an individual process, whereas experience in the traditional sense was – in its manifestation as much as in its modalities of turning into memory – more of a collective work: the experience of old people, for instance, was the voice of an entire social group. That said, Benjamin highlights a number of moments in which experience is able to surface: moments of 'profane enlightenment', such as reading, thinking, waiting and walking. They are no less enlightening than opium, dreaming and inebriation, 'not to mention that most terrible drug – ourselves – which we take in solitude' (Benjamin, 2005 [1929]: 216).

Experience, even in the modern age, is activated when it comes into contact with these intermittent springs. Therefore, it is not impossible but a latent possibility. Whether or not this possibility is actualized depends on the will and work of the subjects, that is, on their ability to perceive its absence with discomfort and strive to remedy it.

In the heart of our contemporary social world, there are forces that – echoing Benjamin's thoughts – tend to oppose the end of experience and propose a substantial restoration of its dimensions. This was clear, for instance, in the closing chapters of Marshall Berman's (1982) *All That Is Solid Melts into Air*. The ultimate outcome of modernity, according to Berman, is indeed a critique of its processes and results from the inside, which brings a growing number of people to make the vindication of spaces of experience the object of social battles. Similarly, Alberto Melucci (1996), in *Challenging Codes*, spoke of a critique of the end of experience as one of the contents of new 'post-political' movements. Some traits of this critique are likely to reappear, even in the most recent social movements (Jedlowski and Pellegrino, 2020). After all, even the resort to different forms of psychotherapy – which in recent decades in the West, has reached a scale pertaining more to the realm of cultural phenomena than of psychic pathology – points to similar attitudes and needs (Benasayag and Schmidt, 2007).

The autobiographical space

Among the forces of modernity, perhaps as a counterweight to the tendencies contributing to a crisis of experience, is a huge increase in what we might call the 'autobiographical space', that is, the growing presence of autobiographies and autobiographical discourses. This increase has distant roots. One of the many paradoxes of modernity is the fact that the individual's interest in the past appears to be weakening while, at the same time, becoming more urgent than ever. The causes of this paradox lie in the importance the individual has acquired through the modern age. At its onset, in the Renaissance, this emphasis primarily meant a reclaiming of the authority of individual consciousness based on experience and reasoning, against any pretence of authority based on tradition. In later centuries, this emphasis took on different forms and motivations but remained a central part of the culture. The emergence of autobiography as a literary genre, starting in the 1700s, would be unintelligible without taking into account the new meaning that the idea of an individual existence, limited by death but inherently dynamic, has come to possess in society.

An individual recognizes itself as such both because it is able to differentiate itself from others and because it can recognize its own continuity in time. The importance of these processes should not be understated. They require an individual to be able to look at their own life as a biography. Things, however, are contradictory: social complexity multiplies the others with which we can compare ourselves, and change causes discontinuity. These contradictions are the soul of the urge to talk about ourselves: we need to do it precisely because it is increasingly difficult to recognize ourselves.

This is not a mere increase in literary biographies. In the introduction to his *Le Pacte Autobiographique*, Philippe Lejeune (1975) observed that autobiographical writings are only a part of what he defined as 'autobiographical space': the complex of novels, letters, oral conversations and so on in which, in different but complementary forms, the impulse to relate our lived experience finds expression. Later, Lejeune looked into self-narration in the context of interviews (not only on the radio and on television but also in sociological research), studying diaries, exploring the autobiographical potential of cinema and highlighting the fact that even in ordinary conversation, each one of us, one way or another, ultimately talks about ourselves. These various modes of autobiographical discourse are not independent from each other but cooperate with each other. They are part of a never-ending effort to define ourselves that is expressed in different occasions and forms. It is as if people today were all engaged (some more, some less) in a sort of constant autobiographical project.

Indeed, in recent decades, the bookstores have been swamped with biographies, and in more recent years, they have been joined by countless autobiographical writings from the web, self-produced videos and selfies. Autobiographical writing in the 1900s became widespread partly as a response to the need for emancipation voiced by marginalized groups (think of the importance of feminist autobiographies or the role of autobiographies written by African Americans in the US). However, its pervasiveness today, while not entirely alien to these needs (the desire to 'have a voice' of those who feel their voice is denied), seems to have mainly other causes. It is not inappropriate to recall Christopher Lasch's (1979) hypotheses on the 'narcissist society' and to observe that the search for validation from others through insistent self-presentation has recently become a real passion for 'visibility' (Brighenti, 2015). In a competitive social world pervaded by audio and visual media, visibility matters, and the autobiographical discourse can be instrumental to it. However, there are probably deeper needs at play, related to the necessity not only to present ourselves but also to recognize ourselves, or even to search for ourselves. These needs are a consequence of the discomfort caused by the difficulty to reflect what we experience today due to the business of our lives, the fragmentation of our experiences, the difficulty to collectively deal with the issues pertaining to the meaning of life and perhaps even the need to oppose the dizziness caused by the perception of our infinite smallness in a world that strikes us for its overwhelming proportions.

At least for some, the autobiographical discourse seriously engages memory and responsibility. For instance, in the very recent autobiographical film *Marx può aspettare* by Marco Bellocchio (2021), one of the most notable Italian directors of our day, Bellocchio, now in his 70s, examines the suicide of one of his siblings (his twin brother) over 40 years earlier. His entire family is involved in the enquiry. The motives of that suicide remain unclear, but what is clear is that everyone, to a certain extent, has tried to cast it aside. The conversations are emotionally charged. In one of them, the director says: 'When someone you lived with for twenty-nine years, your own brother, your twin even, does something like that ... Well! I really didn't understand anything!' *I did not know anything*: this is the conclusion of memory work. However, this conclusion modifies the identity of the narrator, or what he thinks about himself; it pushes him to look to life and even history in a different way than he used to; and it moves him to a new sense of responsibility.

This film presents a unique case: autobiographical discourses are always used by the subjects to locate themselves in collective time (Brockmeier, 2000), though not necessarily through processes of this depth. Nevertheless, the autobiographical discourse always has some impact on the future.

Introducing a monographic issue of the review *Memory Studies* dedicated to this theme, the editors state that 'memory serves to connect individuals not only to their pasts but also to their futures' (Schacter and Welker, 2016: 242). In the articles contained in the issue, this statement is confirmed by several studies on amnesic patients: those who 'have trouble remembering events from their past also have difficulty imagining their own future' (Merck et al, 2016: 286). There are differences between those who struggle with episodic memory only and those who are impaired in their semantic memory: semantic memory normally resists longer, at least in patients affected by dementia or Alzheimer's disease, enabling them to project into the future if not the image of certain events, then at least the schemes by which a future can be understood. Either way, the relationship between mnestic capacities and representations of the future is extremely close.

Those who intentionally attend to their autobiographies are normally not amnesic patients. However, even for them, there are some obvious links between past and future. First of all, an autobiography often features the recalling of previously imagined futures (to evaluate them, for instance). Interest in the future, however, is a constant underlying theme in these writings. As noted by one of the most well-known animators of autobiographical writing groups in Europe, Duccio Demetrio (1995: 95, our translation): 'The time of the tomorrow enters the autobiographical process and fills it with expectations.' At least in our imagination, we write an autobiography with an intention that it will be preserved.

Nostalgias

We write an autobiography to make peace with the past; sometimes to get rid of it; sometimes to keep it close. When we want to preserve the past, a particular theme can emerge in the autobiographical discourse: the theme of nostalgia.

Nostalgia is a feeling involving the desire of a past that we consider lost. It can be a place, a person or a time. In any event, the object is associated as much with the idea of loss as with a desire. This desire can be explicit or undetermined: what nostalgia declares is a deficiency of the present, or a lack, which is given a shape by images from the past.

At the literary level, modernity has always had a close relationship with nostalgia. However, in recent decades, once again, this feeling has acquired a different weight. From the 1970s, a whole film genre emerged: 'nostalgia movies'. One of the earliest and best-known examples was *American Graffiti* by George Lucas (1973). However, almost every country has its nostalgia movies. Beyond cinema, the developments of this tendency led Zygmunt Bauman (2017) to dedicate his last book to what he has called 'retrotopia': a sort of collective inversion of utopia, as if beauty could now only be found in the past. Almost at the same time, Bulgarian writer Georgi Gospodinov (2022) made a novel out of this same idea in his *Time Shelter*, the story of a huge collective experiment in which all the peoples of Europe, frightened by the future, decide to go back to live in the past. Each group chooses its favourite historical period. Then, costumes are picked, cities are brought back to their old architectures, language, media and political systems are copied from the past, and they start living in this reconstruction.

Returning to the past is not a good idea. Concretely, it is impossible. Moreover, nostalgic memory is often deceitful: it beautifies the remembered object, forgetting its flaws. Gospodinov's novel ends in disaster. However, nostalgia can take different forms and perform different functions.

This is perhaps the simplest and the most common function: if the object of desire is out of reach, nostalgia can act as a compensatory mechanism. In other words, it can be a way of recognizing that some desires cannot be satisfied, but this does not mean that they should be completely betrayed and removed; rather, we can preserve them and express a certain loyalty to them.

This is due to the fundamental ambivalence of nostalgia. In the same moment in which it recognizes the distance of its object of desire, it builds a sense of closeness with it, or, at least, a relationship: a bond is forged and maintained with what was lost. Thus, two ends are reached at the same time: the present is recognized as missing the object of desire; but the object is also kept close to the subject, in their imagination.

Nostalgia, then, may hold the solution to a typically modern problem. Modernity is not just the age of fleeting time; among other things, it is also the age of the excess of possibilities. We have many reasons, and many different identifications are available to us, as well as multiple projects of action; we can contemplate different and oftentimes conflicting desires. This abundance is also a potential source of dismay, uncertainty and distress. However, by contemplating the possibilities that cannot be actualized (we only have one life after all), nostalgia can enable a balancing between contrasting desires. Nostalgia shows that it is not necessarily, or completely, a matter of choosing between these desires: while we live one life, we can still be loyal to a different life in our imagination. In this sense, nostalgia is the compensation for a particular kind of loss: the loss of unexperienced possibilities with which we are bound to live as modern men and women.

However, nostalgia also has other functions. These functions match the two forms of nostalgia identified by Svetlana Boym (2001): restorative nostalgia and reflective nostalgia. The former invites the return to, and the reconstruction of, an original home. The latter accepts loss, confronts it and invites us to elaborate its grief. This elaboration implies a self-critical moment. The object of nostalgia is often embellished by the feelings surrounding it, but reflective nostalgia does not remove the ambivalent or negative aspects of the recalled past. It has a critical attitude: it does not take the embellishments of memory at face value.

The fact that nostalgia can lend itself to critical and self-critical discourses has been discussed in several articles published in another issue of the review *Memory Studies*. Presenting the issue, the editors note that nostalgia in modern history has been used for mainly reactionary purposes. Nothing, however, prevents us from considering it as a tool for 'shaping and directing historical consciousness' (Atia and Davies, 2010: 182). The thought inspired by nostalgia can be critical, or even subversive; in some cases, it is the form taken by the memory of subordinate, marginalized or defeated groups.

This re-evaluation of nostalgia should not surprise us. In an age in which the ideology of progress is abundantly showing its cracks, nostalgia for what this process has led us to lose clearly has its appeal. However, we believe that nostalgia, in itself, is neither critical nor reflective, nor restorative, nor anything else; rather, everything depends on how it is interpreted, that is, how its force is used to confront the past. Basically, nostalgia is an alienating feeling. It is not a reaction to displacement (though it can be) as much as a displacing force; it exposes the present as a time we are unfit for. Estrangement – *ostraneniye*, as Boym explained referencing Victor Šklovskij's formulation of this concept – is a sharp and intense perception of the world, that is, an act of distancing that inspires wonder. As alienation from the present, nostalgia is the perception of an absence and, at the same time, the opening of a possibility. Its way of pointing at the object of desire in the past can be false, but its pointing at a desire is authentic. In this sense, nostalgia, once again, speaks to the future.

Memories of the future

The intertwinement of memory, future and desire is especially obvious in a specific type of memory: the memories of the futures we once imagined – probably the object in which the relations between memory and future studies are most apparent (Jedlowski, 2016). As we will see in more detail in Chapter Two, there is a circularity between future and present: the present produces the future through the actions we perform, but the future, as anticipated in the imagination, also produces the present, as the way we act is determined by our anticipations. The anticipations present in each given moment compose the 'horizon of expectations' described by Koselleck (1985); this horizon refers to what is not yet but, because it is perceived, is also part of the now.

The horizon metaphor is fitting. As Luhmann (1976: 140) wrote: 'The essential characteristic of an horizon is that we can never touch it, never surpass it, but that in spite of that, it contributes to the definition of the situation.' The fact that it contributes to the definition of the situation we are in means that it is part of our sense of acting in the present, or orienting it.

This set of expectations is not necessarily consistent; rather, it can simultaneously engage different temporal extensions and is anything but stable. It varies between different social groups, and it is made up of non-homogeneous elements, comprising predictions, projects, ambitions, aspirations, commitments, hopes and fears. It is shaped by impulses and opportunities offered by the real world, but what matters is the subjects' capability to interpret these. It includes the expectations outlined by institutions, as well as the visions of the future summoned by political manifestos, works of fiction, advertising and the arts. Public and private discourses contribute to it. It imbues our daily life. Every society, every group and every generation has access to, and builds, different horizons of expectations.

This is the horizon we find ourselves summoning when thinking about memories of the future – the horizon we used to contemplate in a present that is now past. We can make it explicit by giving attention to it, but every memory implicitly contains the trace of the horizons of expectations in which past events took place (Husserl, 1964 [1928]). These traces can be brought to light; this is the essence of memories of the future.

The autobiographical discourses we discussed in the previous section often evoke them. Every retrospective definition of our identity normally includes questions and affirmations about the futures we have progressively deemed possible. The comparison between these futures and the ones we actualized makes much of that work of reconciliation with one's own history that pervades the deepest autobiographical discourses. However, identity and past futures can also have more superficial – but still important – links. To cite a literary example, think of the character of Mrs Pocket from Dickens' (1993 [1861]) *Great Expectations*. Her identity, in her speeches as much as in those of anyone who knows her, is repeatedly defined based on 'her poor grandpapa's position'. Her grandfather had not been aristocratic, but he *could have* become one; therefore, she could have been one as well. The fact that she did not is marginal; what counts is that the field of possibilities she experienced in the past is a solid component of her current identity. Her memory of the future is important to her. We find this mechanism in many different instances: in the identity of someone who could have been a sport champion, did not become one, but continues to structure their identity around that possibility; or in the identity of many former militants of a revolutionary movement that might have been defeated or have disappeared, but whose hopes remain the centre of the self-representations of its members for the rest of their lives (Traverso, 2016).

A link between identity and past hopes is often present in collective identities. Collective memories can express themselves through the visions, aspirations or programmes of previous members, or of those of which the group claims to be the heir. The regret of a future that could have been can sometimes result in the political use of nostalgia, but past projects are also often recalled by discourses forging the identity of revolutionary movements. Walter Benjamin (1968 [1940]) stated that every revolution is heir to all the oppressed of history, remembering the violence they endured and calling for their revenge; it is a memory of the future that the victims were denied, or an appeal to what that future could have been but was not.

Mentioning Benjamin enables us to widen our scope, as in his works, the past is actually full of hope (Szondi, 1978 [1961]; Marchesoni, 2016). As Benjamin (1968 [1940]: 254) wrote in his 'Theses on the Philosophy of History': 'The past carries with it a temporal index by which it is referred to redemption.' In other words, putting to work the memories of the future, one can end up seeing the past not only and not as much as a collection of 'not-anymores' but also as a reservoir of 'not-yets' (see also Bloch, 1986 [1947]): a repertoire of unrealized possibilities that we can tap into to inspire the present and our future actions.

This thought, beyond Benjamin, drives the reflections of all the authors of the Frankfurt School. The revisiting of promises and potential contained within the past can lead to the reactivation of the desire that used to animate them. Moreover, it is perhaps the ability to project desire on to the future that we feel with the utmost urgency today, at least in the countries we still consider 'advanced'. Our drive towards the future appears weakened, which is probably where the major interest of our theme lies. Our memory of the futures we expected in the past can be tasked with reactivating this drive. Even the memory of past utopias, as much as it must necessarily include a critical moment, can perform a similar role, as we shall discuss in the following chapters (Jameson, 2005; Levitas, 2013).

However, the Walter Benjamin quote we referenced earlier deserves to be remembered in its entirety:

> The past carries with it a temporal index by which it is referred to redemption. There is a secret agreement between past generations and the present one. Our coming was expected on earth. Like every generation that preceded us, we have been endowed with a weak messianic power, a power to which the past has a claim. (Benjamin, 1968 [1940]: 254)

The first part mentions redemption; outside of theological language, and considering the context in which Benjamin writes, it primarily means that the past talks about the future of the oppressed and demands their vindication. The secret agreement between generations mentioned in the second sentence is an allusion to this, but there is more: the fact that we were expected on this Earth, as Benjamin writes, also points to a specific responsibility we carry, a responsibility to remember what we had been promised. Furthermore, the fact that every generation has been endowed with a certain messianic power means that every generation has the ability to hope and some chances to fight so that these hopes come true. We hope and we remember the hopes of those who came before us on Earth, and by hoping, we, in turn, become their heirs.

We can remember the violence endured by others in the past and become the heirs of what others have hoped. Either way, the memory of past futures speaks of the difference between what has been and what should be. In this sense, it always expresses a sort of criticism towards the given present.

We will return to the topic of the relationships between generations referenced in the quote in Chapter Three, but for now, to complete our point, we need to add that the memory of the futures we imagined in the past can be misleading when we do not also employ its specific skill, which is the knowledge of how things actually played out. It can be true that memory keeps a trace of the hopes, promises and potentialities that were betrayed, but it is the present that can and must evaluate how and why they were betrayed.

Not all the futures imagined in the past deserve to be reconsidered, and even for those that do, the present cannot forget what it knows about what past visions could cause and the unintended outcomes that resulted from them. As we will discuss later (see Chapter Two), reviewing the futures within the great narration of 'progress' is useful precisely for what it brings to the analysis of the realizations of progress. Such an analysis is required for any new future projection. Memories of the future are not only useful to redeem unrealized potential; they also help us recognize our past mistakes and responsibilities. A memory that neglects to consider the heterogenesis of remembered ends is mutilated of one of its essential parts.

Globalization and memories

What memories of the future ultimately teach is that the expected future was never singular. By showing that the past is a receptacle of possibilities, however, they suggest the same thing about the present itself. We might say that they can make us retrospectively recognize unexplored possibilities, and we would once again be faced with the estranging strength that memory can sometimes manifest: it enables us to imagine the future beyond the ways in which we most obviously anticipate it based on the established common sense.

The investigation of memories of the future intertwines different research fields. It belongs to the study of time experience, but it also has political undertones: remembering the futures we expected in the past reopens the spectrum of possibilities, gives momentum and provides critical and self-critical tools (Wilson and Jaffé, 2017).

Certainly, for some, the memory of unrealized hopes can cause melancholic attitudes. Melancholy is a memory that keeps the future in check; it is the attitude of those who reject the present and think nothing could have been, and therefore can ever be, different – often combining this attitude with a resentful vein. Resentment, today, is a very common feeling (Tomelleri, 2015), originating more from the perception of some relative deprivation and less from memory. However, memory, carefully manipulated, supports it. This is what happens today, according to Paul Gilroy, to numerous members of the white middle-lower class in the UK. For these people, Gilroy (2005) has coined the term 'postcolonial melancholy', a mixture of nostalgia for the lost empire and aggressive depression, capable of harbouring racism and violence.

Widening the scope beyond Europe, the legacy of the colonial period appears to be itself permeated by violence. For formerly colonized people, activating memories of the future can mean, above all, remembering stolen futures, or, at least, futures that were forcibly transformed. In general terms, we must remember that violence breeds violence, and memory is ambivalent in this regard, for it can breed feelings of revenge as much as attempts at reconciliation.

This problem involves all the pasts that in one way or another can be defined as traumatic, painful or controversial. The existing authoritarian regimes certainly do not favour their emergence if not in instrumental ways, but the 21st century began with an immense multiplication of historical memories. Beyond specific local cases, this is one of the general consequences of globalization (Inglis, 2016). Global communication today gives a voice to countless versions of history. This is a positive fact in many ways, but these memories often contradict each other. The recognition of histories and memories considered local or marginal until today is not the only thing at play. This matters and must be greeted with favour, but the fact that these memories can include contrasting representations of shared events is equally important – and problematic. In the heart of Europe today, this fact is obvious in the difficulty to accept the coexistence of the memories of individuals who lived under different regimes. Every conflict entails the construction of antagonistic memories. The memory of the violence endured by the losers challenges the memory of the winners and can generate or legitimate more violence. It is difficult to prevent this outcome, but the 21st century will have to live with the plurality of historical memories.

This coexistence might have to involve a partial unravelling of the relationship between identity and historical memory, or, at the very least, its rethinking. It is true that, at an individual as much as at a collective level, memory is a function of identity, both in the sense that it is what enables a subject to recognize itself as the same through time and in the sense that identity is the selector that causes the subject to prefer certain memories to others. However, unequivocally connecting memory to identity can make us forget that memory is also what can contradict the identity a subject intends to assume in any given moment. On the individual plane, psychoanalysis has shown how one of the points of interest of memory lies in its capacity to preserve the traces of even what could *not* be incorporated in the development of consciousness, thus escaping the processes of constitution of an identity; this is the reason why memory always has a destabilizing role. However, this is true even on the collective plane: memory is not merely what serves the 'good identity' of a group and its interests; rather, it is also a repository of traces that can fuel its self-critique. We cannot be proud of everything we have done. However, the capacity to not hide it and to take responsibility for it makes all the difference: it allows for a circulation of recognition between ourselves and others that insistence on past wrongs does not permit (Ricoeur, 2004).

The studies on memories of the Holocaust remain exemplar. In part, the issue is how to pass down this memory to the next generations so that they can recognize and combat the insurgence of similar phenomena. However, at the same time, it is about recognizing what about this memory is enduring, often in implicit and silent ways, but not less relevant for the lives of the descendants of victims and perpetrators (Rosenthal, 1997). Whether we are aware of it or not, the actions and traumas of previous generations impose themselves as a burden on the lives of later generations. What matters is a dimension that is at once individual and collective: what the predecessors recount and how, as well as what and how the successors can pose questions, regarding what concerns the descendants not just of the victims but even of the perpetrators (and we should not forget how these two roles can sometimes be overlapped or reversed [see Morag, 2013]). The past cannot be changed, but its interpretation can, and so can the service memory provides to the future: against the interpretations of the past that push us towards revenge, we can build memories for which the past is no longer the entity holding the future hostage.

Media and new media

Individual and collective memories coexist and influence each other. In any event, everywhere in the world, neither individual nor collective memories are intelligible without referencing the role played by the media in their formation.

The media as a whole contribute to the social construction of what each one of us means by 'reality'. However, what is socially constructed is also the reality of what belongs to the past. Press, radio, cinema and television have done this for all the 1900s. Given the relatively small number of broadcasters existing then compared to the present, many of the representations of the past provided by news articles, films and television programmes dedicated to history were able to reach huge audiences. If states were no longer able to grant a common historical memory, the job was done by television and film. However, due to the expansion of the offer, audiences gradually diversified. Those who read a given newspaper or follow a given television channel, and those who consume pay-per-view programmes or choose a DVD to watch at home, do not form similar historical memories because the materials used to build them are different.

In recent years, this diversification of audiences has received intense contribution by the new media. Films and television programmes in the central decades of the 20th century could aim at audiences that coincided with whole nations; if they talked about the past, they were contributing to the edification of the historical memory of a whole country. The new media have unpredictable, less stable and usually segmented audiences; this segmentation is caused as much by the exponential growth of the offer as by the new and various possibilities of initiative of the users. Mediatic events of ample (national or supranational) resonance are still possible, but due to the quantity and speed of the different stimuli each theme has to compete with, every topic runs the risk of having a short life (Affuso, 2010).

The effects of the media on the formation of historical memory are still important today, but they are more scattered than they were even a few decades ago. The link between individual and collective memories has become thin. The notion of collective memory is meaningful only as long as there is a recognizable group with some stability through time. In a world in which offline and online interactions are mixed, different groups form, consolidate and disaggregate incessantly, so that talking about groups is less appropriate than talking about social webs: sets of relationships that can be activated more or less sporadically, each time in response to different needs, without creating anything like a common identity.

The place of – at least potential – confrontation between different collective and reticular memories is what sociologists call 'public memory'. This is the ensemble of images of the past that, at any given moment, not only circulate among certain groups of people but are also regarded as publicly relevant and are publicly discussed. It is memory as an object of the public sphere. By definition, it is an open space, the space in which different memories communicate (or clash) with each other about the criteria of selection, plausibility and relevance of the past, while also exposing themselves to criticism from other memories.

The new media would appear, at first, to revitalize the dynamics of public memory: they involve a democratization of the public sphere that gives space and voice to a plurality of memories that would otherwise be confined to the private sphere. However, we must also note that this democratization has proven to be easily polluted by organized interventions (think of the diffusion of fake news). Even when there are no manipulations, the excess and fragmentation of discursive flows that characterize the Internet limit the impact of each and every single voice, often confining them to a presence that is not only temporally ephemeral but also limited to groups of users whose ability to interact with others can be so scarce that they greatly limit the 'public' character of these memories: the reciprocal segregation of the webs animating these memories can be so extensive that it generates what some call a 'balkanization' of the public sphere and, therefore, of memory itself.

All of this happens simultaneously to what should be regarded as the highest impact of the Internet: the exponential growth of social memory. If by 'social memory', we mean the collection of all the traces of the past preserved within a society (Namer, 2000), then it is clear that this collection is expanding in new ways today. It is an archive (or, better yet, a multitude of archives) of extraordinary proportions. It has immense potential, but it also poses some problems. Too much, sometimes, can amount to nothing. An archive has little meaning without criteria of classification and organized mechanisms of retrieval. Beyond the technical issues (especially the rapid obsolescence of informatic language systems), the issue lies in the classification of what is contained in the archive, as well as in the managing of retrieval activities; these are delegated to search engines, whose functioning defies the competence and action of each user. This effectively configures an occult dominion of the retrieval function by those who manage the engines.

Therefore, the Internet and new media as a whole seem to have caused not only a huge expansion of what is memorizable but also a fragmentation and, in some ways, a progressive evanescence of what can be defined as memorable. In this context, individuals search for new ways to relate to memory and the media themselves. In their daily lives, they seem to increasingly rely on the constitution of 'light memories' (Mandich, 2010) externalized in portable devices in which the choice of preservable materials is primarily tied to their personal activities and daily relationships, and where materials from the most disparate sources are mixed.

However, we should be cautious in making clear-cut diagnoses. The web is also the most favourable environment for the emergence of what could be called 'memory currents'. This expression refers to traces of the past that survive in the recesses of social memory and lend themselves to being re-actualized by subjects in unexpected times and places. It is a sort of unused reservoir that gathers contents specifically tied to 'values that were excluded from the center of society' (Namer, 1997: 271). These contents can be encountered and re-actualized by individuals or groups. It is almost a karstic memory. Flowing between different times and places, these contents can become a part of the historical memory of individuals or groups that are not necessarily in touch with each other, establishing new and significant links between the past and the present.

The digital revolution is likely going to be seen as an epochal change in the future. However, these kinds of changes take time to unfold and are difficult to decipher while they are happening. For the moment, what it seems to be producing is a huge extension of what is memorizable and a corresponding decrease of what is memorable for individuals and groups. What is important to remember? Since media users today seem to move at times in droves and at times in absolutely singular ways, the answers to this question change rapidly and can be various. The past, however, can hardly be called silent.

A partial conclusion

The emergence of the Internet, computers and, more recently, smartphones and similar devices belongs to the history of the expansion of the human ability to exteriorize memory through technological supports. Throughout the modern age, technologies have offered increasingly powerful tools to preserve and reproduce traces of the past. Cultural attitudes in this regard have been and remain contradictory. On the one hand, modernity represents a recurring crisis of traditions, which leads to a devaluation of the past. However, modernity is also the age of original institutions and activities, such as museums, restauration and antiques, and of the diffusion of a feeling like nostalgia. It is also the age of autobiography: a literary genre that embodies an attention of subjects to their own biographical past, which, as far as diffusion, has no precedents in history.

What has most defined the relations between modernity and the past is the emergence of a keen awareness of the distinction between present, past and future; it is only because of this awareness that the past lends itself to a specifically historical knowledge that is attentive to chronology and dates. This awareness seems to have been fading since the early 21st century. Many have seen this as a relevant cultural change. However, historical memory is not necessarily 'historical' in the modern sense of the word; rather, it is a relation of meaning between the past, present and future that can prescind from verifiable chronologies and can be found in every human society, ultimately originating in the cults of the dead (Assman, 2011 [1992]). This observation should make us sceptical of characterizations that paint our time as an age 'without memory'. The fear is real, but some sort of relation between the past, the present and the future is consubstantial to humans.

'Presentism' – the marked accentuation of the present, or the almost exclusive concentration of our attention on the present – is a trait of the modern condition, but there are counterthrusts to it. These are seen in individual attitudes expressing desire and the ability to navigate time, but they can also be recognized in collective attitudes. The unconditional adhesion to the present plays the game of several economic and political interests. It is akin to an ideology, and like an ideology, it can be contested. Within public memory, social movements are relevant actors: they elaborate alternative attitudes and memories, and fight to propose their importance to others.

Our time is ambivalent towards memory. On the one hand, memory is a political and biographical theme whose importance is not decreasing; on the other hand, the speed of change reduces interest in the past. These two tendencies exist at the same time. Meanwhile, the huge increase of social memory and the multiplication of views on the past make the choice of what should be considered memorable difficult, or at least fragmented and always contestable.

Memory studies do not seem to be decreasing in importance. Many disciplines take part in them. Philosophy, psychoanalysis, psychology and social science are joined today by the contributions of neurosciences (Kandel, 2006). The extension of the duration of life implies, among other things, an increasing relevance of age-related memory disorders, motivating significant funding to research on this theme from the pharmaceutical industry.

However, memory concerns everyone. It is neither a medical issue nor a mere education issue because it does not simply involve knowledge of the past; rather, it requires us to confront certain elements of it and – in the more successful cases – to transform them in constitutive moments of what could be called our 'experience'. In this regard, the main impediment is perhaps the acceleration of life. Living rapidly, we go through many experiences and might be unable to keep anything in mind, but this means being unable to orient ourselves.

The impossibility to confront our experience ultimately coincides with our inability to confront our legacies: the legacies we leave to ourselves and others through our lifetime, and the ones others have left to us. We always inherit something: we inherit the conditions in which we find ourselves living; we sometimes inherit material possessions; and we always inherit some cultural elements. Whether we are aware of this or not, we will always have to deal with what we inherit, and awareness enables us to make certain choices. This goes for any legacy – even the ones to which we attach a negative value. Memory is a meaning relationship built between the present and the past; it is the choice of what should be kept in mind while proceeding towards the future.

TWO

Futurity: Changing Futures in a Changing World

Between past and future

Hannah Arendt, the scholar who made public action the heart of her reflection, directly references temporality to denounce the crisis wrought by mass society on the construction of being-with-others within the public space and, therefore, of political action in general. More specifically, Arendt evidenced the unbridgeable discontinuity between past and future produced by the demise of tradition – which is understood as a tradition of 'opening up to the world along with others'.

Published in the US at the beginning of the 1960s, *Between Past and Future: Six Exercises in Political Thought* (Arendt, 1961) collects reflections elaborated between the mid-1950s and the early 1960s. The book openly expresses Arendt's acute discomfort regarding her present, marred by the loss of the collective memory of the struggle for liberation from Nazism. With the fracture in memory, not only does the past fade into uncertainty but the present also ends up lost in the crisis. Lacking resonance, past and future drag the new generations towards a meaningless horizon.

Chapter One ended, significantly, with a reference to the legacies – good or bad – left by each generation to the next. These legacies are shaped by memory and can be infused with energy and transformation potential by expectations of the future. Chapter Three will focus on generations as a critical junction of the materialization of time, sitting at the centre of the transition between past and future.

This transition is at the heart of Arendt's book. In fact, the preface to the book is titled 'The Gap between Past and Future' and opens with a metaphor quoted from French poet René Char, who was part of the French Resistance movement. Proposed by Char in the last year of the Resistance, between 1943 and 1944, the quote reads: '*Notre héritage n'est précedé d'aucun testament*' ('Our inheritance was left to us by no testament') (Arendt, 1961: 4). According to Arendt, this metaphor is meant to convey the difficult relationship between past and future when the inheritance received is not legitimized by any tradition (the testament). A testament, as we know, connects the past and future together through an act of will, thus granting the continuity between what was and what will be for what concerns the use of certain assets. Char's present, like that of the other member of the resistance who were, like him, intellectuals turned to action, becomes a present of crisis, a present that is no longer legitimized by their past. This happens because 'concert action', that is, acting with others (their shared past as freedom fighters), is abandoned, which leaves them blocked in a privatized present. As a result, the future itself, which is undetermined by its own nature, cannot be open to intentional change. In summary, Arendt is signalling the importance of a political reflection capturing the interrelation between what was and is confronted by memory – the roots of the present – and the flux of change.

The crisis of the present, which the book touches upon and is hinted at by Char's metaphor, should not, however, overshadow another key aspect of Hannah Arendt's thought. As is well known, in her vision, 'natal time' – the time of a new beginning, of politics seen as an unpredictable phenomenon – is an essential part of the world's change process. From this perspective, the turnover of generations can combat the crises of the present by forging new and unprecedented forms of acting-with-others. The non-individualistic conceptualization of the crisis points evidenced by the present can transform them in resources for action. In this framework, the future, which Arendt certainly sees as being as distant from the ideology of progress as much as from the temporizing utopias of the 1800s, can be understood as a tangle of open possibilities.

If we transpose the method proposed by Arendt to deal with the discontinuities of her time to the present day, we need to take as our starting point the historical character of futurity – our theme in this book. The modern conception of the future as an open and progressive time will thus become the necessary starting point of our reflection, as on this basis – by understanding 'where we come from' (Jedlowski, 2016) and, thus, what we left behind us – we can gauge the width and depth of the temporal transformations faced by our present. Today's presentism is a consequence of the crisis of the future related to the dissolution of the modern model of historicity (Hartog, 2015), as well as to the digital revolution and to the cultures of instantaneity that characterize our time.

It is not new, but it is clearly more and more the case the deeper we delve into the new century that talking about the future amounts to discussing a political theme. At the centre of this debate – along with the redefinition of the world's geopolitical map, including a war at the doors of Europe; with the energy crisis, as well as the now-intolerable level of economic and social inequalities both among different countries and within each country – are the serious threats facing our planet as a consequence of the global environmental crisis. It is especially the new generations, whose future is tied with a double thread to the evolution and pace of this crisis, who have made the ecological problem a true political issue, loudly asking the great powers' elites for a quick change of course. In this framework, such movements as Fridays for Future have become the symbol of the struggle against a temporal economy built around the rejection of all limits (Pellizzoni et al, 2022), as well as of active forms of responsibility towards the yet unborn (Jonas, 1984).

Caring for the future, in particular, for the long-term future, is acquiring a centrality never before seen in human history and turning into a real object of political battle. The generic preoccupation with an uncertain future has transformed into a new, scientifically informed awareness of the mortal threat looming over our planet's future and the various species that inhabit it. The separation between the times of nature and the times of society (Chakrabarty, 2021) – which is the basis of modernity – has turned on its creators: a new temporal age has begun, calling for a radical redefinition of social times, from the commodification of time to the identification of time with profit.

Time cultures

Before we analyse more directly the transformations undergone by future representations throughout the generations – especially the particular representation we usually identify as modern – we need to take a closer look at the type of social and symbolic constructions of these expressions of time. As social constructs, collective conceptions of the future transform throughout history, clearly bearing the imprint of the different cognitive epochs of humanity. This term alludes to the different ways of understanding the universe, nature and the existence of human beings. Depending on its collocation in these various cognitive epochs, the subjective experience of time also changes. The changing nature of the various visions of the past, present and future offered to us by history are directly tied to this process.

We can, then, say that the different levels of knowledge of human beings also shape their ways of being in the world, which are expressed through temporal orientations. As Norbert Elias (2007 [1985]) has made clear, temporal consciousness is not a biological or even a metaphysical datum but, rather, a cultural and social dimension that changes according to the different stages of development of social contexts and the ways in which collective activities are organized within them. This intuition had already been expressed by Durkheim at the beginning of the 1900s.

According to Elias, as we know, the experience of time referenced by modern common sense – an objective reality flowing 'out there', outside of the perceiving subject, and measurable by clocks – is the result of a difficult evolution, spanning multiple centuries, related to the development of human knowledge. This evolution is characterized by a trajectory moving from concrete to abstract. Basically, as the modes and forms of knowledge change, the ways of relating to, understanding and living time also change. The more complex societies become, the more temporal concepts tend to abstraction and to a higher degree of conceptual synthesis. The time of nature and stars that used to coordinate human activities in pre-modern social organizations gives way to the abstract and empty time that disciplines the rhythms of manufacturing and, later, industrial labour (Tabboni, 2001). The time that in the world of tradition, was inseparable from action and its contents morphs into a time with no qualities, usable and monetizable, a *conditio sine qua non* for the application of machines to human labour (Agamben, 2007 [1978]).

In this process of progressive abstraction, the way of understanding and relating past, present and future is also transformed based on a similar tendency, according to which social attention gradually moves from the concreteness of the present towards the future, a time that is not immediately experienceable. As for the past, it is actualized through the cult of elders and thus absorbed into the present.

In short, in archaic societies, the immediate present – the here and now – guides collective and individual action. In these societies, the flowing of time from the past to the future follows a cyclical scheme: everything that was will be again, only an interval separates the past from the future. The old is contained in the new.

As we know, archaic thought makes no distinction between present and future, so much as between sacred and profane time (Eliade, 1959). Sacred time, through celebration and ritual, allows the reproduction of the original time – mythical time. Profane time is a time of preparation for the irruption of sacred time into social life. Sacred time determines temporal rhythms, separating the symbolic areas of the magical and extraordinary from the areas of everyday life. In this concrete temporal universe, measured by concrete events, centred around the present, episodical and reversible, sacred time is both a grantor of the world's continuity and the instrument through which death can be defied.

What is completely missing from this temporal scenario is the idea of the long-term future. Beyond what happens in the immediateness of the close environment, there is a curtain that prevents us from 'seeing' time, perceiving it and wondering about its meaning. Beyond the here and now is the vast realm of legend and myth that can only be accessed through ritual, divination, prophetic dreams and oracles (Adam, 2004). Powerful and mysterious forces that regulate the life not only of human beings but also of gods inhabit that space.

The separation between what was, what is and what will be becomes clearer and clearer as the need to account for the very distant future increases. This transformation happens, as we will see in more detail in the following paragraphs, with the onset of the modern age. In the coordinates of modernity, the centre of time – and thus of human action – becomes the future. It is the future that influences what humans do in ordinary and extraordinary circumstances; the future is the stakes, the risk and the challenge that social collectivities and individuals have to face. The idea emerges that human beings can become the arbiters of worldly history and time: history is appropriated from the transcendental world; and time is tamed through the project.

Towards the open future: the premises

We cannot study the modern paradigm of progress and its deep influence on the construction of modern temporal horizons – which we are gradually abandoning in our present age – without lingering, even briefly, on the 'epochs of time' that have historically preceded modernity. Specifically, we are referring to the Christian order of time that has been laicized by modernity. The vectorial character of this temporal order presupposes a starting point (the Genesis) and an endpoint (the Apocalypse). Christian time derives its light and meaning from the birth of Christ. As we will see, in its secular and modern version, this time is robbed of its transcendental character and deprived of every other meaning other than the structuring of an independent before and after (Agamben, 2007 [1978]).

Unlike the Greek concept of time, in which the cyclical dimension still prevails and the dance is led by the mythical past, Christian time no longer identifies the past as the 'guardian of time'. While they notoriously made a distinction between *Chronos* as a continuous and quantitatively measurable time-flux and *Kairos*, a qualitative time suggesting the idea of an opportunity to be seized, the ancient Greeks were still immersed in a cyclical notion of time (Ricoeur et al, 1975). Like Benjamin's (2002 [1936]) 'angel of history', propelled towards the future by a storm that pushes their wings against their will while their gaze turns to the past, the ancient Greeks seem to be walking backwards towards the future, remaining essentially focused on the past.

Once again, fate is the entity that governs time: its law rules over humans and gods. The resulting perception of time is inevitably static and distant from the idea of human control over time and history. In ancient times, the same political forms cyclically return, following a predetermined order. The Eternal Return dominates the horizon.

The disruption of this temporal image is tied to the spread, after a long and complex process, of the Judaeo-Christian view of time. According to this view, time moves not circularly but linearly. Earthly time (*tempus*) and eternal time (*aeternitas*) are conceptually separated, opening the first space for a representation of time as an entity that can potentially be controlled by humans.

It is true that modern time will have to wait until the 18th century to affirm the new 'regime of historicity' (Hartog, 2015) that radically redefines the relation between past, present and future. However, the Christian temporal order lay the foundation for this redefinition: just as the past is no longer the centre of time (as it was in the Greek world), neither is the future alone, following the Jewish vision expressed in the Old Testament (Ricoeur et al, 1975). Past, present and future are all fully inscribed in the ceaseless flowing of time between the two poles of Genesis and Apocalypse. At the centre of this flow is the advent of Christ. The vectorial image, later inherited and transformed by industrial society, is dominant: we come 'from', and are headed 'towards', the last day of the world. Faith is the grantor of the meaning and unity of this path.

As the antithesis to the cyclical view of time, the Christian temporal order affirms that whatever happens only happens once: it is unrepeatable and loaded with meaning. On the one hand, time acquires historical consistency for the first time, becoming the arena in which free will finds an expression; on the other hand, human participation in history is not seen as an end in itself but derives meaning from being part of a divine design that both transcends and includes it. The primary actors of this time are God, who holds past, present and future in their hands, and God's people, the Christian community as a whole – never the individual. In other words, the idea of the future, like the idea of history, becomes a property of humanity exclusively in virtue of the fact that humans are divine creatures.

Nevertheless, this view is the first to assign a purpose to the time of Earth dwellers and to appreciate its value. The flow of time is not mere chronology, nor is it the inertia of an endless return. Time, in its three dimensions, becomes creative potential. The future, especially, becomes more important than the present, the ephemeral time par excellence. In this eschatological temporal horizon, the time to come is identified with salvation. The future of human beings has a supreme and insurmountable limit: it is closed by the Apocalypse, the endpoint of history.

Christian time, then, is fundamentally dramatic – and not only because of this extreme limit. Within this temporal horizon, life on Earth is represented as a space in which the forces of good are engaged in an eternal battle with the forces of evil. The transcendental context in which life on Earth is inscribed is the basis of this view.

The new historical time and the future

Modern time (*Neuzeit*) re-elaborates this representation, freeing it from any transcendental references and using it to kickstart the new industrial organization of labour. Worldly progress takes the place of spiritual perfection. According to Koselleck (1985, 2018), this shift replaces the doctrine of universal judgement with the risk of an open future – which is also an opportunity. The fracture between past experiences and future expectations, a key concept of the semantics of historical time proposed by Koselleck, which is typical of modernity, starts here. This fracture is a result, first of all, of the acceleration of change brought about by the secularization of time.

In the agricultural world, processes of social change were slow and tied to generational turnover. When they were quick and abrupt, they were not self-determined (such as famines, floods or other catastrophic natural events – the irruption of wars is another example). The experience of older generations was a valuable asset because it enabled society to make reasonable predictions about a future that would probably not be excessively different from the past. The profound transformation of humans' relationship with history, which is the basis of the idea of an open future, has drastically erased this type of temporal economy.

For the first time, the future is removed from the double influence of nature and the divine, becoming subject to human dominion. Consequently, historical time opens up to a mixture of opportunities and uncertainties. In human and social sciences, as Barbara Adam has rightly noted (Adam and Groves, 2007), this transformation also gives special relevance to the assumption of responsibility for historical events by human groups, as well as single individuals. It is no coincidence that both these concepts – an open future and responsibility – are both proposed during the Enlightenment (Ricoeur, 1994).

The new time of modernity, then, breaks down the idea of limit – any limit – to human presence in the world, a stance that can revolutionize political orientations as much as daily behaviours. This idea, as highlighted by Luhmann (1976), had a deep and pervasive influence on the schemes of modernity for at least two centuries.

With the image of a divine plan for humanity long gone, the future now appears to be tied hand in glove to the choices and decisions of the present. This link between present and future applies to societies as much as individuals. In a nutshell, an increasingly future-oriented universe supplants the 'traditionalist' universe that preceded the French Revolution. To put it in Pomian's (1980: 9) effective words, the gravity centre of time is moved. As a new gravity centre, the future influences collective action, making room for biographical projection on the individual plane. As a consequence, unlike our predecessors, 'we live leaning towards the future, keeping our balance thanks to the movement caused by its attraction power' (Pomian, 1980: 9).

In this scenario, novelty, discovery and innovation are pursued for themselves. In economics, science and technology, and even art and literature, the opening of the future releases time from its powerful bond with past experience. This is when the idea of progress as an irreversible, infinite force took shape, as we are about to discuss.

However, before we delve into this pivotal step in the construction of the modern temporal order, we need to make one last observation on the opening of the future, which is directly tied to the issue of generations. This theme is expressly mentioned by Krzysztof Pomian in his article on the concept of future developed by the Enlightenment age and its crisis (Pomian, 1980; see also Pomian, 1984: esp 291–302). Among the various consequences of the 'temporalization of history', which has led us to see the future as shapeable by human action, is a different conceptualization of life stages. Thus, starting from the 17th century, childhood becomes socially visible (Ariès, 1962) as a past-less but future-rich time, or in the 19th century, the 'discovery' of youth coincides with its valorization as the depositary of new world views and lifestyles. The new centrality of these social ages coincides with the progressive marginalization of old age, which is seen no longer as the valued keeper of memory but, rather, as the very emblem of decline.

Lastly, on a more general level, we need to note that the demise of the transcendental perspective forcefully restates the problem of the finitude of human time in this historical period. The importance of the generational perspective, starting with the turning over of generations within the family, enables us to anaesthetize the anxiety caused by a secularized worldly time that ends in the individual's death and to project ourselves beyond the present through the mediation of future generations. This process is especially visible in the context of family time. Whereas family time had always been mostly past oriented (ancestor worship is an obvious example), its temporal orientation is also modified. Now, the family identifies the future, rather than the past, as the strategic perspective to preserve its identity. Memory of the past is fertilized by hope in a better future for the younger generations. This orientation has a direct expanding impact on temporal horizons.

Progress and modernity

Freed from the shackles of tradition, the future becomes a time to be dominated and moulded according to the determination to better the human condition, or to make humans happier and freer on Earth. While up until that point, the experiences of generations past and the transmission of their knowledge through memory had been a source of security and guidance for the present, a new perspective began to emerge. Interestingly, the moderns become the 'new elders', whose actions and knowledge we can take as a useful reference for collective life. Only a historical mirage might have led human beings, until then, to see the knowledge transmitted by a remote past as valid. That knowledge was actually childish, and the sparse useful pieces of information had been led on the wrong path. That false authority that had been transmitted through the older generations had to be wiped out forever.

The realization of this strategic process depends on the affirmation of a radically different world view able to open unthinkable social and political horizons and foster unprecedented expectations. We might say that modern time is born as a result of this revolution. The 'religion of progress' feeds this revolution and gives it credibility. For this reason, the decline of the religion of progress following the waning of the idea of the long-term future as a dimension open, by definition, to continuous and irreversible improvement (Taguieff, 2004) radically transforms contemporary representations of time.

The link between the modern concept of progress and the construction of modern temporal horizons is, in fact, crucial. While the 19th century is the true 'age of time' (Conrad, 2018a), the age in which time becomes a central category for daily life, as well as for science and the arts – the names of Einstein and Proust immediately evoke this process – the foundations for the new temporal order were laid in the previous century.

As Koselleck writes, referencing the temporal revolution of the 18th century and the effects of this revolution on the notion of historical time, '[t]ime does not just remain the form in which all stories take place, it gains a historical quality itself. History then no longer takes place in time, but through time.

Time is dynamized into a force of history itself' (quoted in Nowotny, 1994: 86–7). As Bury (2014) had already observed in his 1920 book on the idea of progress, this idea seems to be unable to develop without the new concept of time as a linear continuum, lacking any inherent qualities, which characterizes modernity. The representations of time and progress, both seen as limitless, run parallel to the increasing expectations around the future and the continuous betterment of the human condition – which are also seen as limitless. This parallel transformation can no doubt be regarded as the quintessence of modern experience. For this reason, we often hear that the opening of the future, together with the 'temporalization of redemption' allowed by modern progress (Taguieff, 2000: 243), enables the simultaneous rejection of the religious world view, with its closed time, and the cyclical world view of the natural universe. We will return to this last aspect in a short while.

In this framework, the distinction between the modern view of progress and previous views throughout human history is crucial (Koselleck, 2006). While Nisbet (2017 [1980]) claims that long before the Enlightenment, there were ideas of progress with analogous transformative power – for instance, among the ancient Greeks and Romans, as well as in the later Middle Ages (and, from a philosophical perspective, in Augustine's work) – Koselleck holds a different view. In his eyes, the idea of progress is not entirely absent in pre-modern times, but it refers to specific and partial progresses in particular scientific fields, such as physics, astronomy or medicine, as well as in art or in politics. However, it is not an actual 'movement of history' towards control of the future, as is the case with modern progress. A reflection on the new temporal regime in which the latter idea took shape can help us understand the strategic differences between the two.

It is only from the 18th century on – when the idea of progress establishes itself as a comprehensive social process – that the link between time and nature is broken up for good. The reference to the rhythms of nature, the movement of planets and the cyclicality of processes of growth and decay seem to be the residual of a different historical phase that belongs to the past and is now devoid of meaning – which must therefore be quickly left behind. In other words, the new ideology prevents even remotely considering the idea of decadence, which is inseparable from natural processes. Thus, new temporal horizons open, in which the standardization of time, now abstract and uniform, will begin to play a vital role.

The modern idea of progress, tied as it is with the task of freeing humankind from the shackles of superstition and absolutism – a task, as we have seen, that is understood as irreversible and unstoppable – cannot but wipe away all previous representations of time. However, it must be stressed that the characterization of time as empty and progressive associated with this project does not altogether exclude the possibility of struggles and setbacks. Nevertheless, while discontinuities cannot be completely ruled out, they will become a stimulus towards further conquest and progress thanks to new scientific knowledge and the mastery of the laws of nature it enables. In this framework, optimism about the future, once merely an option, becomes a necessity.

The open and 'long' future of this temporal outlook has a direct impact on the relationships between generations. Human happiness, substituting the importance previously reserved to salvation, is finally within reach: the generations who grasped this extraordinary truth must take charge of passing it on, shouldering any present hardships. The final goal, the realization of the project of a freer, and therefore happier, life for everyone, justifies this sacrifice (Bury, 2014 [1920]).

The new way of experiencing the world suggested by these representations of time gives the utmost importance to time projectuality, through which the uncertainties that necessarily accompany the opening of the future can be kept in check. We may say that from a functional perspective, projectuality becomes the modern equivalent of magic in archaic societies (Bergmann, 1981). On the individual plane, however, the logic of projectuality paves the way for the modern constitution of identity: the life project becomes the organizing principle of biography.

It is only an apparent paradox that the problem of death emerges simultaneously with the human conquest of the future through the new, progress-shaped concept of time. Leaving behind the transcendental horizon, modernity postulates 'an infinity of time in a universe *that is indifferent to human existence*' (Spencer, 1982: 686). 'Securing' the future by planning it thus becomes the most rational way to ward off the anxiety inevitably caused by this finitude. In this new scenario, freedom and uncertainty seem to be inextricably linked. In a way, we can say that the greater capacity for future planning made possible by the rise of the idea of progress on a social and political plane conceals an attempt to 'defuturize' the future, purging it of its specific traits of indefiniteness, of openness to possibilities, as well as to risk.

For at least two centuries, this attitude towards the future persisted and the ideology of progress, despite the changing scenery, did not lose its power. It was only after the two world wars that the myth of progress and the controllability of the future through planning were heavily challenged, as we will see in more detail in the second part of this chapter. The narrative of the modern conception of time was severed, allowing the hegemony of an increasingly defensive attitude towards the future. This process would bring the redefinition of both the present and the past, along with the forms of memory itself. The roots of what we now synthetically call 'the crisis of the modern representation of time' must be traced back to this temporal revolution.

What is, then, in this scenario, the future of the idea of progress of which we just analysed the genesis? Should we abandon it for good, or can it be reformulated in light not only of the happenings of the 20th century but also of contemporary priorities (Wagner, 2016)? To answer these strategic questions, however, we need to complete our reflection on the idea of progress, touching upon a rarely examined problem: the role played by the ideology of progress in the rise of European colonialism (Fabian, 1983; Conrad, 2018a). This ideology would differentiate and hierarchize non-European societies and cultures based on their ability, or inability, to adhere to the principle of progress as the indispensable prerequisite of development. A society was considered backward if it did not perceive itself as part of this 'mechanism of history'; its members were considered 'inferior' if they did not accept the linear temporal regime, grounded in a mechanical notion of time that accompanied that world view.

Thanks to the ideology of progress, European superiority to these societies and people was taken for granted. What is more, indigenous people appeared to colonialists as living relics of ages past – as 'contemporary ancestors' (Nisbet, 2017 [1980]: xiv). For this reason, during the international expos that took place in European capitals in the 1800s, indigenous and aboriginal people from various continents were 'put on display'; they had the unparalleled ability to turn back time. By the same logic, several ethnographic and ethnological museums in the 1800s framed the encounter with different civilizations as a 'journey back in time'.

We can thus say that the emerging world order and the capitalistic organization of time that encapsulates it, which is increasingly apparent with each passing decade, use the ideology of progress as a tool to destroy autochthonous notions of time. This imposes the abandonment of natural rhythms and of the prevailing cyclical temporality of colonized societies: entering the process of 'civilization' requires, for instance, leaving behind mythical representations of the past.

In short, the revolution of time, which is functional to the new forms of social disciplining presupposed by the transformation of labour organization, imposes the standardization of time and the construction of a new spatio-temporal order on a global scale. In this framework, temporal horizons undergo a radical change. The concept of social acceleration aptly expresses the direction and developments of this change (Rosa, 2013).

Futurism: between the celebration of the future and the myth of speed

Social acceleration is certainly not just a contemporary phenomenon. Modernity was characterized by the acceleration of change, meaning the 'abbreviation of the periods which allow for a homogeneity of experience' (Koselleck, 1985: 252). By the mid-18th century, according to Koselleck (1985: 257), 'the technicizing of transport and information made acceleration a temporally specific datum point'. In the early 19th century, the perception that time 'slips away' was already widespread, and '[t]hat which then went at a steady pace is now at the gallop' (Arndt, quoted in Koselleck, 1985: 252). This process radically redefines the relations among past, present and future: the past seems to be an increasingly remote dimension, while the future acquires the features of a challenge. Newness is the feature that most connotes the present.

The spectacular technological innovations that took place between the mid-19th century and the First World War – from the internal combustion engine to the inventions achieved by applying the laws of electromagnetism, for instance, electricity generators, electric motors, the telephone and the telegraph, and then the invention of the cinema and the rapid development of railway transport – gave body to this new *zeitgeist*. While unprecedented ways to interpret space and time spread in physics as well as in psychology, the arts and music, the collective experience of time and space underwent profound transformation. As a consequence of the increasingly rapid circulation of goods, people and information, and the relative reduction of the distances among places, the pace of life intensified (Berman, 1982).

To be stressed here is that this acceleration process was primarily functional to capitalism's demand for the more rapid circulation of capital and information. As Marx (1993 [1857–58]) pointed out in *Grundrisse*, reducing the time necessary to conclude transactions was an essential requirement for the affirmation of capitalism. The progressive standardization of time imposed by the spread of railway transport, which culminated in 1910 when time worldwide was synchronized from the Eiffel Tower in Paris (which emitted a radio signal that could be picked up over a range of 5,000 km), attests to the progressive subjugation of space by time:

> It is most disagreeable that one cannot now-a-days learn a thing once for all, and have done with it. Our forefathers could keep to what they were taught when they were young; but we have, every five years, to make revolutions with them, if we do not wish to drop altogether out of fashion. (Goethe, quoted in Conrad, 2018b: 836)

In the famous novel *Elective Affinities*, written in the first decade of the 19th century, Goethe makes his protagonist Eduard pronounce these words, also expressing the unease of adult and elder generations particularly, who unwittingly found themselves living in that tourbillon of change and technological, artistic and cultural innovation that characterized the transition from the 18th to the 19th century.

As masterfully highlighted by Kern (1983), along with the enthusiasm for the new opportunities created by the growing presence of technology in transportation, communication and what would today be called *loisir* ('leisure'), new worries also emerge. In Goethe's novel, Eduard is referencing the issue of the obsolescence of acquired knowledge – 'every five years', he says, knowledge must be updated, so to speak, to keep up with the changes happening in the modern world – a process that can only be intensified by the approaching of the 20th century.

However, this is merely the tip of the iceberg. The acceleration of change in daily life, from the knowledge that supports its framework to the temporal structures that enable its reproduction, ends in a paradox. The more the adhesion to the various innovations tied to the belief in unstoppable progress becomes common sense, the more a past guided by established habits that can be effortlessly controlled can be mythized. In this framework, at least for part of the population, the life of past generations – as it is distant in time and no longer reachable by the present – can be represented as a sort of golden age. We will return to this point in a short while, as we discuss the 'invention of the past', which is symmetrical to the exaltation of the future as the time of newness. Both the invention of the past and the exaltation of the future are products of the 19th century.

We now wish to draw attention to an artistic movement of the early 1900s known as Futurism, whose *Weltanschauung* ('world view') is completely at odds with this mythization of the past. Its aspiration was actually to burn down and destroy the very symbols of the past, starting with museums and the liturgy of memory they celebrate.

In the context of our discussion, the importance of Futurism, a movement that encompasses and connects a variety of artistic expressions, from poetry to painting, from sculpture to applied arts, from architecture to music, from cinema to theatre, lies in its ability to conjugate a total love for the future with a profound adoration for speed. Future is the emblem of the new and unprecedented, the time of conquest and pleasure: 'Why should we look back, when what we want is to break down the mysterious doors of the Impossible?', wrote Marinetti in *The Founding and Manifesto of Futurism*, published in Paris in 1909 (Rainey et al, 1999: 52). Speed is seen as irresistible energy, the force through which we can move beyond the anachronism of a society seen as still too oriented to the past: 'We affirm that the world's magnificence has been enriched by a new beauty: the beauty of speed. A racing car whose hood is adorned with great pipes, like serpents of explosive breath – a roaring car that seems to ride on grapeshot is more beautiful than the Victory of Samothrace' (Rainey et al, 1999: 51).

The increasing speed is attributed first and foremost to the movement of people and goods thanks to the ever-more powerful machines available to the elites: at the beginning of the 1900s, these are the 'roaring cars' exalted by Marinetti and the other futurists; later on, as predicted by the *Manifesto*, comes 'the sleek flight of planes' (Rainey et al, 1999: 53). The religion of innovation and acceleration embraced by Futurism is undoubtedly a prerogative of the young generations: 'The oldest of us is thirty: so we have at least a decade for finishing our work. When we are forty, other younger and stronger men will probably throw us in the wastebasket like useless manuscripts – we want it to happen!' (Marinetti, quoted in Raney et al, 1999: 54).

In the Futurist vision, it is precisely the 'new' generations who are living this constant change almost as a new obligation, as a torment. 'Modernizing' the world becomes the new buzzword. In this sense, human speed and technological speed support each other. 'Human speed' refers not only to the acceleration of the movement of human bodies through space but also to the acceleration of thinking and judging processes, and to the growing inclination to experimentation. Recklessness, attraction to danger and, more generally, the non-conformist scenography showcased on a daily basis are nothing but side effects of the feverish search of a fast pace under the existential profile. Machines support this quest for freedom from tradition and social constraints, showing the path to the liberation from stasis and to the new experiences made possible by scientific discoveries and the technologies embodying them.

From a strictly artistic perspective, the 'artificial' aesthetic of the mechanical world is deemed by the Futurists to be superior to the traditional aesthetic, which was strongly tied to the past. The fact that the founder of the Futurist movement, Filippo Tommaso Marinetti, was Italian, with Italy being the proudest of its glorious artistic past among nations, is a paradox worthy of its age – a paradox that pointed out the trend of the new century to the intellectual, cultural and artistic world in the decades preceding the First World War. Fascism would appropriate, and in part exploit, this tension. Indeed, from a historical perspective, Futurism has often been understood as a precursor of fascism: an aversion to liberal ideology, a rejection of traditional authorities, a glorification of war and a contempt for women are the traits that unite these two movements the most.

Returning to the years in which Futurism acquires its distinctive cultural profile, which is completely outstretched towards the future – between the end of the first and the beginning of the second decade of the 20th century – it is important to stress its glorification of every form of originality: primarily artistic, though also scientific, social and political. It is on the basis of this search for originality that the *Futurist Painting: Technical Manifesto* (Boccioni et al, 1910: 4), put forward in 1910 by the most relevant group of Futurist artists at that time, while declaring its preference for 'a whirling life of steel, of pride, of fever and of speed', proclaims '[t]hat the name of "madman" with which it is attempted to gag all innovators should be looked upon as a title of honour'. In the machinist utopia in which this group moves, along with Marinetti, it is most important to make room for individual genius, for incendiary creativity and for the capacity for action in the here and now (Braun, 2004).

In conclusion, as always – and even more probably in the case of Futurism – it is fundamental to frame currents and cultural movements in the historical times that generate them. The glorification of movement and speed takes place in an age in which industrial development, especially in Italy, is at its peak. A few years earlier, at the end of the 1800s, Frederick Taylor had started to publicize his own method of scientific management of industrial work. As we know, for Taylor, it was essential to speed up production in its every facet and form, cutting 'waste' and 'dead time' – another declination of the passion for speed that characterizes the turn of the century.

And what about the past?

As we saw earlier, the 'futurization' of time, then, becomes the distinctive trait of the modern temporal order. The acceleration of change at the roots of the ideology of progress, which is also an acceleration of the rhythm of history at the hand of human subjects and of these subjects' own lifetimes in relation to their personal objectives (Blumenberg, 1986), follows this process. However, as Felipe Torres (2022) rightly underlines, the modern temporal regime coordinates and connects not only progress and acceleration but also even a utopian spirit. Torres re-elaborates all these concepts, which had previously been explored by Koselleck (2006) mainly in *Begriffgeschichten*, devoting special attention to utopia. In Torres' reflections, utopia is seen not only as a conceptual tool that is strategic to rethinking the future as a horizon open to possibility – that direction of history the ideology of progress never ceased to praise – but also as a 'structural condition' able to exert a profound influence on the meaning and transformation potential of the future. In the following pages, we will examine how each of these aspects is rethought and refined in contemporary modernity.

However, in this scenario of 'futurization', what is made of the past? Why can we affirm that the past, as we understand it today, can be seen as a literal 'invention of modernity' (Conrad, 2018a)? As we have already said, since the Enlightenment, history has stopped being conceived as a repetition of past events. Rather, emphasis is put on the possibility to use it as a medium to discover the unknown, the unexpected and the unthought of, in other words, what can be seen as antithetical to tradition. In this framework, according to Aleida Assmann (2020: 36–7), diverse histories set in a plurality of contexts, concrete and local histories, or 'histories of something' are replaced by a singularization of history. This singularized history is in a way sterilized, running along a linear and empty time that becomes a framework for all possible histories. In a word, history, thus conceptualized, becomes a regulative idea that can guarantee a principle of order to the world's incessant flow.

The side effect of this emphasis on progress is a sharp separation between the past, present and future. The disconnect between these dimensions is deliberately pursued and seen as an instrument of freedom – even liberation. The past is identified with oldness. It is, quite literally, 'outdated': 'Something from which one can definitively turn away' (Assmann, 2020: 52). According to Aleida Assmann, modern historiography is centred around the idea that the past can no longer 'communicate' with a world that sees newness as the source of meaning. In the modern universe, which is increasingly focused on the future, the prevailing temporal culture ends up pushing history to exclusively focus on the past.

As Sebastian Conrad (2018a) has shown, in many societies around the world, as time measurements become standardized through the adoption of an abstract, decontextualized global time, interest in the past as the potential bearer of different times and lifestyles grows. In Europe, this reduction of the past to a long-lost dimension causes two different, but interrelated, reactions: a sort of nostalgia for pre-modern worlds and social times (Lowenthal, 2015); and a strong push for the museification of history and memory.

Nowadays, one of the challenges encountered in the transmission of historical memory through generations is preserving the meaning of this transmission while temporal horizons are contracting. Hence the tendency of contemporary Western societies to devote almost obsessive care to the preservation of remains and to the memory that makes them come alive – a task facilitated by ever-more sophisticated virtual aids. In other words, the memory of a sterilized past that is purged of its conflictual and identity dynamics tends to assume greater importance the more our future horizon appears bleak.

However, we need to be aware that this transition from viewing the past as a dimension of life and history, at once full of teachings and, by definition, supportive of the future, to viewing it as a 'dead time' disconnected from both present and future happens in a social and cultural context that is altogether different from the one in which we live today. The past, enclosed and protected in neutral spaces like museums, and the very idea of a cultural heritage to be carefully preserved – as long as it is decontextualized – become visible when trust in the future is at its peak. The founding of the Louvre Museum in Paris right after the start of the French Revolution can be seen as emblematic of this process.

'*Si le passé est separé de l'avenir, l'esprit marche dans les ténèbres*' ('As the past has ceased to throw its light upon the future, the human mind wanders in obscurity') reads a famous quote by Tocqueville (quoted in Chesnaux, 1996: 275). The present cannot ignore the past, but it cannot hide in the past either. Nor can it run away from the future. Presentism, which we are going to discuss, faces a political issue of great significance, which can be summarized by the question: can the democratic societies of our time do without the future and the past, and opt to live exclusively in the present?

Presentism and the threatening future of the 21st century

'Memory is a meaning relationship built between the present and the past; it is the choice of what should be kept in mind while proceeding towards the future': this is the conclusion of Chapter One on memory. The temporal crisis that most evidently affected the last decades of the 20th and the first decades of the 21st century broke the strategic link between past, present and future, giving prominence to the redefinition of temporal horizons.

However, the crisis of modern time, which is centred around trust in the future and the ideology of progress that warrants it, began in a very clear manner in the 1940s. That temporal web, which had taken several centuries to form, was shattered by two traumatic events. The Shoah, as Bauman (1991) has magisterially shown, challenged the possibility of viewing the forms of Western rationality as a protection against barbarity and genocide; while the explosion of the atomic bombs in Hiroshima and Nagasaki destroyed for good the non-belligerence between human time and Earth time (Hartog, 2022). Thus began the dramatic process that led to direct confrontation with the irreversibility of time – a crucial theme to reconceptualize the temporal horizon in our era. When we talk about environmental emergency or, even today, of a possible nuclear emergency, we reference precisely this irreversibility.

The human capacity to dominate the world through technology, to the point of potentially destroying life itself, not only challenges the possibility to conceive historical time – that is to say, to take for granted the possibility to relate past, present and future. It also, and even more radically, challenges the relation between present and future. In this framework, the future is mainly viewed as a threatening time: not only does it not bring an improvement of the status quo but it also easily becomes the expression of the uncontrollable. Therefore, it mainly causes fear. This explains the attempt to exorcise this fear by gradually shifting attention towards the present. As we will see in more depth, this is also the start of the rapprochement between the issue of responsibility towards unborn generations (Jonas, 1984) and the necessity to bring the future back to the centre of contemporary discussions on time.

Before we cover these issues, however, we need to identify a few essential moments in the trajectory that lead to the presentism that is so discussed in recent decades. While the crisis of the future studied by Pomian (1980) at the beginning of the 1980s is an obvious stepping point, today, for those who wish to approach temporal issues in contemporary modernity, we must not overlook another, equally important historical passage. We refer to the three decades between the end of the Second World War and the oil crisis of the early 1970s, a period in which, in several European countries (as well as others, such as Canada), the social and economic worlds were swept by a wind of optimism. Those were the years of the post-war reconstruction and of the widely held belief that after the horrors of the war and of totalitarian regimes, it was finally possible to nurture the amount of security that is indispensable for development and peace – a confidence that the future can be better than the present. Even the Cold War, with its menacing hold over geopolitical relations, could not undermine this feeling of hope. The Cold War did leave an ambivalent mark on the post-war image of time. Besides the construction of new and vast temporal horizons, shaped by optimism, this formally unarmed confrontation rang an alarm bell to the belief in a future with no shadows. Indeed, as we know, the idea of a future open to innovation and well-being was about to begin to dim and fade. Since the oil shock of the 1970s, and with progressive acceleration, thinking about the future mostly tends to generate an increasing unease. However, for a handful of years, the idea of the future remained a positive idea. It is telling that so-called 'futurology studies', built around the perspective that the future can be prefigured and made the object of adequate technocratic investments (and therefore, potentially, controllable), started to develop in those years (Gidley, 2017; Andersson, 2018).

A constellation of elements contributed to peripheralize the idea of the future as a positive force after this short period. Among the main ones are: the loss of history's end directedness, which deprives linear time of purposiveness; the marked expansion of the realm of the possible, accompanied by the perception of the increasing likelihood of uncontrollable social and ecological risks; and the perception of living, in more than one way, in an unpredictable age (Martuccelli, 2017), reinforced by the 'assaults' of forces that were thought to be part of the past – viruses and war. COVID-19, for instance, has imposed not only heavy losses but also deep devastation in the economic and social landscape, as well as unthinkable redefinitions of social relations. The war at the doors of Europe, triggered by the Russian invasion of Ukraine in February 2022, also brings into focus the association of future and threat, as well as the idea of a past that does not pass: a blocked time that locks us into an accelerated but directionless present. In an increasingly interdependent world, these events and processes undoubtedly levitate our fears and prevent the future from reacquiring a benign profile.

The colonization of the future by the present begins in this context. To put it more precisely: although the evocation of the future continues to constitute a routine, both for social systems and for subjects, it is in fact the present that is now associated with the principle of governability and controllability that modernity, through its normative ideal of progress, associated with the future.

Inevitably, given the temporal structure of action, this future's uncertainty impacts on the modes of social action, as well as on identity construction. With growing pessimism as to whether the future can be governed, the devising of medium- to long-term biographical projects is increasingly pointless. In classical modernity, not only did biography and project – in the sense of a life project – presuppose each other but collective and individual projects were two sides of the same coin. The objectives of the former – liberty, democracy, equality, economic well-being and so on – were the preconditions for the achievement of the latter. In this tension, social plans and individual plans jointly contributed to constructing biographical profiles for which the past–present–future nexus, namely, the dimension of continuity, was crucial. Identity, in its turn, took shape around this integration.

We can borrow from Claude Lévi-Strauss (2020 [1962]) the concept of bricolage, a device from magical and archaic thought, in order to bring into focus the particular cognitive style that drives contemporary tendencies to construct project-less biographies. For Lévi-Strauss, a bricoleur is someone who performs work with their own hands, using tools different from those of a craftsman. What is striking about the bricoleur is their ability to adapt to the materials available and to construct the equipment needed step by step. Without a specific project, the equipment is improvised. No element of the whole on which the bricoleur acts is tied to a predetermined use; the outcome of the work depends on the conditions and the means present here and now. The results of the work are therefore, by definition, contingent. Furthermore, the initial intention is likely to be extraneous to the final product. In a certain sense, the bricoleur, guided by an essentially practical logic, personifies the separation between rationality and intentionality.

Melucci (1989) has evoked the figure of nomadism as a metaphor for contemporary biographical trajectories, especially among the youth. The 'nomads of the present' do not pursue a specific goal; rather, they wander/explore, enwrapped in provisionality. They are not concerned with the idea of a frontier, the idea that ties space and time to something lying ahead and that, as such, must be 'faced' (Cassano, 2012). Frontiers have been thrown open in the global world. The nomads of the present can roam aimlessly among unconnected places: waystages in their biographies whose connections are identifiable on the basis not of a project but of reflection ex post. The long-term memory that extends beyond the personal lifetime, as well as being projected into the non-immediate future, tends to remain silent. Time fragments into episodes, each with its own self-referential temporal system.

The biographical construction that emerges in this context gives priority to the present, isolating the person from both the past and the future. Identities, in turn, tend to transform into 'situational identities' (Rosa, 2013): instead of being conceived as the result of the relationship between what was, what is and what will be, these fluctuating identities almost bring us back to pre-modern realities that are actualized by the great amounts of contingency that characterize the uncertain modern landscape. As Rosa (2003: 19–20) observed: 'This "new situationalism" in a way resembles premodern forms of existence in which people had to cope with unforeseeable contingencies on a day-to-day basis without being able to plan for the future.'

In this respect, it may be useful to briefly reflect on the two distinct temporal landscapes that have seen two generations into their adulthood (Leccardi, 2012): the baby boomers (born between the end of the Second World War and the mid-1960s) and the so-called 'millennials' (born between the early 1980s and the mid-1990s). For the former, the future is a positive dimension, not only in their personal anticipations but also in their social experiences. Thanks to the distinctive *zeitgeist* of their time, their biographical constructions are distinguished by hope, as is their collective future. Consequently, within uncontracted temporal horizons, the future is experienced as a time of exploration and opportunity. The millennials' experience is the polar opposite. In the Western world, millennials are arguably the first generation who grew up in a social climate of growing presentism and acceleration. The construction of, and the control over, biographical time, then, has had to come to terms with the new temporal fragmentation, often accompanied by feelings of temporal anxiety. Of course, this anxiety did take shape in different ways and forms according to the different structural constraints with which these young people had to come to terms, the characteristics of their family backgrounds and the economic, social and cultural resources at their disposal. However, according to different European studies, this negative feeling towards the long-term future seems widespread today (Leccardi, 2017).

Basically, for the young generations growing up in the new century, an increasingly risky future challenges the traditional paths to adulthood and requires the construction of new life patterns (Wyn et al, 2020). For instance, if temporal horizons are shortened, the relationship with institutional times has to be rethought; new forms of agency, able to cope with rapid changes, are needed. In this scenario, the everyday can become the most appropriate ground to express autonomy, while innovative biographical timelines are shaped.

But what do we mean, exactly, by 'biographical time'? As we have seen, this term refers to the unitary temporal dimension that emerges from the processes by which people consider the past, live the present and look to the future. Biographical time and identity are closely bound up with each other – nor could it be otherwise. Personal identity, just like time of lifetime, is the outcome of the dialectical relationship between permanence and change, between continuity and discontinuity. Since it takes shape on a terrain delimited, on the one hand, by the subject's need for autonomy and, on the other, by one's need for recognition, passing through a delicate mixture of identification and dissociation, the raw material of personal identity is, by definition, time, both existential and social (Luckmann, 1993).

It should be stressed in this regard that the possibility of conceiving a dialectical relationship between time of lifetime and social time is itself considered a historical product of modernity. In fact, it was modernity that offered a representation of time consonant with a conception of the time of lifetime as (auto)biography (Leitner, 1982): an abstract and empty dimension within a temporal flow depicted as linear and irreversible. Paradoxically, the 'subjectification' of time embodied in the concept of biography is one of the outcomes of modernity's exteriorization and objectification of time, whereby the latter is considered a thing separate from its perceiver, a dimension that flows autonomously, and is articulated by the unstoppable movement of the instruments used to measure it (Adam, 1995).

This positive relationship between life project, biographical time and identity, however, encounters difficulties when, as happens today, the future is not only foreshortened but also often simply annulled in favour of the present. The term 'presentism' takes shape around this process. However, it is fundamental to distinguish the present as an increasingly central dimension of biographical time (to the detriment of the future) and its transformation in pure instantaneity. This distinction, which is essential to gauge the more recent transformations of temporal orientations, relates to the constitution of instantaneity as a new normative ideal. This process, as Hartmut Rosa has highlighted in his theory on the high-speed society (Rosa and Scheuerman, 2009; Rosa, 2013), is bound to deeply modify social life as a whole.

When the speeded-up succession of social changes, interwoven with the fast pace of technological innovation, is wed to an acceleration of the rhythms of life in a globalized space, even the temporal dimension of the present shrinks. While modernity sees the present as a 'preparation' for the future and abides by its logics, and contemporary modernity makes the present a central time for its self-definition, nowadays, the triumph of instantaneity as the hegemonic cultural reference ends up leading to its contraction. The *Gegenwartsschrumpfung* ('contraction of the present') highlighted by philosopher Hermann Lübbe (2009) and re-elaborated by Rosa, annuls the present as a functional temporal plane for the definition of choices and action. More than a time open to experience – as far as the mutilated horizons of past and future permit – the present appears as a precarious time, in the meaning that Bourdieu (1998) has given to this term. *Precarité*, according to Bourdieu, creates a time without possibilities, in which not only do forms of rational anticipation seem impracticable but there is also no idea of a 'hold' on the world.

At the basis of this difficulty is the present's fragmentation into a plurality of segments with no reciprocal relations, segments that appear as merely de-temporalized surfaces. The shrinking of the present to which Lübbe refers makes the present disappear as a temporal totality, reducing it to a cloud of fragments in movement (Castells, 2000). In other words, the now-capillary diffusion of information and communication technologies, and the cultural hegemony of instantaneity that sustains them, creates a 'de-temporalization of time'. According to Virilio (2000: 76), in these social coordinates, 'we merely abandon the living in favour of the void of rapidity'. In the end, the growing speed of social life of which the contraction of the present can be seen as an indicator produces alienation

(Rosa, 2010) – a condition for a drying up of subjectivity and, along the way, of ethics and politics.

But what are the lines of resistance to the destructuring of temporal experiences linked to this limitless expansion of speed? Here, we want to point at two of these possible lines, both of them tied to social movements. The first line relates to the critique of neoliberal globalization proposed by some of them. The environmental emergency can be seen as one of the outcomes of this dominant form of globalization. The second line is related to the feminist movement and to the centrality within it of daily life as a temporal and spatial realm, in which the plural times of the living make their voices heard. Both movements challenge the necessary loss of future and past generated by social acceleration.

The challenge launched by social movements critical of neoliberalism – today, especially in the guise of climate activists – concerns in parallel the statement of the manifest violation of the rights of the planet and the species living in it, as well as the dominant space and time conceptions behind it. The battle for a cosmopolitan democracy, a goal of at least a part of these movements, asks for a redefinition of concepts like citizenship, sovereignty and political community. This is possible through their capacity to keep together cosmopolitanism and temporality (Cwerner, 2000). This cosmopolitanism seems to be capable of escaping from the shrinking of the global present, the time of cosmopolitan capitalism, in order to look equally at the past and the future: at the past by shedding light on the roots of both contemporary social inequalities and the Western model of dominion over nature and its rhythms; and at the future by underlying the responsibilities of present ruling classes to unborn generations. Here, the planet is profiled like a dynamic system of interconnected spaces and times that have a historically sedimented temporality and spatiality. This cosmos surely receives light from the global present that crosses it, but it is at the same time open to the future and aware of the past; it is constructed by a multiplicity of social and existential times and natural rhythms, indissolubly tangled together. This temporal vision not only refers to ecological awareness; it is also concerned with the search for sustainable development models and the principle of precaution (Adam, 1998). It is again linked to an idea of responsibility broader than the one traditionally conceived by ethics (Jonas, 1984).

For what concerns daily life and the women's movement, the latter has long placed the everyday at the centre of its battle of liberation from patriarchal models of thinking and action. The reasons for this are many (Felski, 2000): first, the close link between everyday life and the space-time of experience (Jedlowski, 1986), or between routine and creativity; second, the capacity of daily life to actively resist dualistic thinking in its various forms (nature–culture, mind–body, individual–social and so on), starting with the opposition between productive and reproductive labour; and, third, its ability to show the close relation between what appears obvious and trivial, as a 'time without history', and the struggle against patriarchy in the history of women (Leccardi, 1996).

In a nutshell, wherever temporality clashes with simultaneity, emerging deeply damaged, there is a chance to bring attention back to a dimension of time that modernity has dismissed: the multiple character of the time of daily life. This time is located at the crossroads of different worlds, both public and private, each with different rhythms, durations and sequences. Within it, social times, natural times and bodily times synchronize through rhythm. Human and non-human animals, together with plants, adapt their own biological rhythms to the planet's revolutions. As we know, the structure of daily time is tied to the physical nature of our bodies as much as to the social constructions that give meaning to our lives. Embedded in daily time, then, are not only personal times or the times of interactions; rather, these times all coexist with physical, natural and social times. This intersection of times sealed by the daily dimension is the basis on which we build meaning. We build memories and images of the future thanks to this intersection.

Although the overall quality of daily time today appears impoverished due to the imperative of acceleration – especially for women with a family and active on the job market (Bryson, 2007) – the feminist movement wants to bring back attention to the irreducible character of this plurality. Women's bodies themselves carry the sign of this multiplicity. The 'far-sightedness' of women is tied to the awareness of generations alternating through time, which, in turn, is connected to women's bodies and their generativity. The battle for the salvation of the planet, which can only lean on the necessity of action here and now to protect our longer-term future, is tied with a double thread to this awareness – as well as to the responsibility, both personal and collective, that derives from it (Pulcini, 2013).

A final thought: rethinking progress

As we considered in this chapter, one of the most distinctive features of our age is the demise of the experience of time that had shaped modernity. The future has lost its aura of promise and grows increasingly threatening. The fading of the idea that the future can be controlled or governed has a clear impact on our understanding of politics. The political system is no longer viewed as a rationally controllable instrument to change the conditions of collective existence.

In this framework, responsibility becomes a form of re-temporalization of action that is able to anticipate the future without being explicitly involved in the construction of a project. It opens the present to the future based on the here-and-now of relational experience. The future is contained, so to speak, in the connection that responsibility establishes, that is, in the 'common time' that it creates. Responsibility shows how the coordinates of social life can be redefined on the basis of what Hannah Arendt called the 'human condition of plurality'. From the recognition of the only partial sovereignty of the individual due to this condition arises the possibility of responsibility.

However, in this analytical framework, it is appropriate to ask whether the centrality of responsibility as a promise that opens itself to the future – it is no coincidence that responsibility and promise share the same etymological root, *spondeo*, answering a request and taking responsibility for something or someone – can deliver a convincing message when it comes to discussing the future of our planet. Here, we are talking not about the time we share here and now but of a time that will be lived by generations we do not, and will never, know.

The need for this new open future – open to an indefinitely extended time to which we need to give a chance to exist today – is happening in the geological era defined as the Anthropocene, an era in which the human dominion of ecosystems is at its highest. As a consequence, nature and society can no longer be thought as separate; on the contrary, their mutual interdependence has grown beyond measure. The climate crisis makes this weaving particularly obvious, forcing us to a global rethinking of time that is similar, as regards its profundity, to the one that occurred in early modernity (Chakrabarty, 2021).

However, in order to take this long-term responsibility, we need new conceptual tools that are capable, in the 21st century, of reopening the future that the growing acceleration has closed again. We need to lay new foundations for our long-term thinking, a necessary premise to discussing the future. Helga Nowotny (2021: 39), using a term created by astrophysicist Stephen Hawking, has talked of 'cathedral thinking' to signify a form of thinking that runs across different generations (thus, across time) without stopping. This is the sense in which we believe the very much exhausted concept of progress can be rethought or radically reconstructed (Wagner, 2016). The direction in which we need to move for this redefinition, however, inevitably requires the assumption of collective responsibility: in the present, in view of the future, taking responsibility for the past.

THREE

Memory and Future through the Generations

Living in different times

Human societies are not static entities that can be studied and analysed outside of time. They can be likened to a train, where at every moment, someone is getting on (newborns and immigrants) while someone else is getting off (the dying and emigrants). How do memory and future interrelate for those who get on and off the train? Where is the train coming from, and where is it headed? Societies must be understood as an entity whose composition is constantly renewing through the succession of generations. What is true of every society is equally, and even more, true of the human population that inhabits the planet like a ship traveling through space.

The concept of generation is widespread. In everyday language, it has a plurality of meanings. It has a bio-anthropological connotation, as 'generativity' (indicating the links of the chain connecting parents and children, grandparents and grandchildren), but it also denotes the fact that being born in a certain period and having lived the crucial years of formation in a certain cultural climate shaped by certain historical events leaves a mark on the way individuals feel, think and act. The fact of belonging to a particular 'time' unites the members of a generation, distinguishing them from previous and subsequent generations.

Both these common notions do not deviate much from the use of the concept in historical and social sciences, where it is frequently employed in two different realms. First, in a demographic sense, we speck of 'age cohorts' to identify the ensemble of those who were born in a particular time period (usually a year). We also refer to 'age cohorts' to denote those who enter school or the military (in those countries that still mandate military service), or even new electors crossing the age threshold at which they acquire the right to vote. Second, in a historical/sociological sense, the word 'generation' identifies the ensemble of those who experienced certain events or historical phases at certain stages of their lives.

A society with many elders and few young people

Let us start with the demographic sense involving the distribution of population in age classes, which sets the framework for a few fundamental dynamics in the relationship between generations. We will consider two groups: people aged 0 to 19 (children, teenagers, and youths) and people over 60 years of age. In every European country, elderly people are more numerous than children and teenagers. In Italy and Germany, there are 1.8 elders for every youth. In France, there are 1.2. In Italy and Germany, the disproportion is more pronounced than in France. The situation is similar in the other European countries, as well as Japan and China, while in the US, Canada and Brazil, this imbalance has not yet manifested with the same intensity. If we turn to the whole world, we find the opposite relation: for every elder, there are three youths. In Africa, 40 per cent of the population is younger than 15, while in Europe, this figure shrinks to less than 15 per cent. In demographic terms, Europe and Africa are at the ends of the spectrum: Africa is young, while Europe is old. All other factors aside, this is going to have an impact on the direction of migratory flows: immigration to Europe may contribute to rebalance the demographic decline, while emigration from Africa risks subtracting a quota of better-educated and more skilled youths from the developmental needs of the continent.

In the history of humanity, there have never been societies with such a high percentage of older people as in Europe today (Livi-Bacci, 1997). Old people are a problem, because their rapid increase has jeopardized the pension and health care systems, whose weight on state budgets has increased correspondingly. Proposals to increase the age of retirement frequently cause divisions and opposition movements: while a part of the elderly population impatiently awaits the day when they can finally stop working, others wish to keep working for a few more years. Meanwhile, unemployed youths would be mistaken to think they can take the jobs that will be freed by the retirement of the elderly: in times of technological change, those jobs are obsolete and thus unavailable to young people looking for employment. The perception of either a conflict or, on the contrary, a commonality of interests between two groups is often quite removed from reality.

This age distribution within the population clearly changes the relationships between generations. In Europe, three tendencies have contributed to create this altogether new demographic situation:

- The decline of natality/fertility rates, which are currently substantially below the level of substitution. This happened (though to a lesser extent) even in countries like France and Sweden, that have implemented natalist policies. The decrease of natality rates affects all countries, with the exception of most of Africa. This is primarily a consequence of the strong and rapid reduction of child mortality, as well as a much slower decline in birth rates. This tendency has enabled women to free themselves, for much of their existence, from the task of ensuring the biological reproduction of society. This happened much earlier in Europe (with differences from country to country), while in Africa, the process began later and is still under way.
- The ageing of the population and, therefore, the rapid increase of the elderly population. The increase in average

life expectancy is clearly the effect – with all the differences from country to country – of improved nutrition and the diffusion of modern hygienic and sanitary practices. This increase, however, was not linear for all societies; in Russia, and in several other countries in Eastern Europe, after the upheavals caused by the collapse of the Soviet Union, the average life expectancy actually decreased for a few years, especially for men.

- The fact that in this historical phase, very numerous cohorts of elderly people have reached old age – the cohorts of the post-war 'baby boom', born until the mid-1960s. This quantitative bloating of the elderly population is bound to reduce in time, with the gradual ageing of younger and younger cohorts. Today, rather numerous age cohorts are still entering retirement, but in forthcoming years, there will certainly be a progressive decrease. If migratory balances were to reduce to zero, the populations of Europe would face an inexorable decline (Golini and Rosina, 2011).

In this historical phase, the quota of population with an objectively short life ahead and a large portion of life behind is increasing: old people have more past than future. For the young population, the exact opposite is true: they have more life ahead than they have behind them. In the societies of our past, and in most of the societies in the so-called 'underdeveloped world', the quantitative relation between generations used to be, and is, precisely the opposite. Few managed to survive to their old age, while young people were much more numerous. Old people were the depositaries of wisdom, and young people were expected to listen to them based on a tradition everyone accepted, rarely daring to question it. This change, it must be stressed, happened in a relatively short time: in less than half a century, natality has dropped by more than half, while life expectancy nearly doubled. These transformations are partly the – not always intended – consequence of public policies, but more often, they are the compounded effect of the actions of individuals and families. In the collective imagination, and in different historical phases, this demographic decline is sometimes interpreted as a negative phenomenon. At other times, it is seen as a positive thing.

Demography is not the only science dealing with generations. For culture and art historians, the concept of generation is used to signal the emergence on the intellectual or artistic scene of new tendencies and styles represented by individuals of roughly the same age, who went through the same formative experiences. The generational approach in cultural and art history enables us to acknowledge the presence of a plurality of different generations in the same period, each of them embodying a different understanding of the literary and artistic expression of their time. Thus, it allows us to escape the rigidity of conventional periodizations that operate through chronological sections. When, for example, we refer to the 1920s' generation to distinguish it from the 1930s' generation, we are using a conventional unit (the decade) that does not match the actual times of change of social and cultural reality.

In sociology and political science, the concept of generation has given rise to interesting research tendencies around the border with historical research. The concept of generation allows us to introduce the dimension of historical time to social research and therefore to limit the abstraction and arbitrariness of many historically undetermined generalizations (Abrams, 1982). Studying society essentially means studying social differentiation, that is, the way society is articulated in categories, classes, groups, parties, factions and so on. Among the various sources of differentiation, age is obviously one of the most important, as every society is characterized by the coexistence of individuals at different stages of their life courses in different roles. Age classes and the corresponding social figures (children, teenagers, young people, adults, older adults and the elderly) are one of the most obvious and commonly studied sources of variability in many social phenomena. The introduction of the generational dimension suggests that it is not enough to know the values, opinions, attitudes or behaviours of the various age classes: the analysis must also determine in which moment or historical phase those individuals lived the different stages of their lives. There is a difference, for instance, between being young in a time of war and in a time of peace, between entering the job market in a phase of recession or expansion of occupation, or between retiring in a time of prosperity or crisis of public finances and social security systems. Individual biographies take shape within a historical context and are influenced and shaped by this context. As Abrams (1982: 293) wrote: 'The problem of generations is the problem of the synchronization of two different calendars: the individual's vital cycle and historical experience' – in other words, the intertwinement of individual and collective histories.

Acceleration transforms the relationships between generations

When human life was shorter and societies changed very slowly, external social reality did not change between the birth and death of a person. Sure, during the course of every single existence, events could happen, both in the public and the private sphere, that could modify, even drastically, one's life path. These could be natural events (such as earthquakes, floods, droughts, diseases, epidemics and so on) or social events (for example, wars, famines, riots, regime changes), but once the perturbation passed, reality went back to its continuity and life resumed its path on the tracks of tradition. Societies changed with time, but they did so through slow processes – through long waves, as Braudel (1995) and Elias (1994) would have put it – and in the short time of one existence, one almost did not notice social change. Generations followed one another, but the world they inhabited remained the same and mostly regulated by the cycle of seasons. This goes not only for all the rural societies of the past but also even for the urban societies of the Middle Ages and Renaissance, which, in this sense, do not represent a real change of direction. It is true that urban societies are inherently more dynamic – as money starts to fuel local and inter-local commerce – but on the other hand, epidemics spread more rapidly in cities and life risks becoming even shorter than in the countryside.

All this changes with industrialization. As Marshall Berman (1982) (an author who was mentioned in the previous chapters) wrote: 'All that is solid melts into air.' Everything starts changing: energy sources, modes of transport, work and production methods, war methods, consumption, housing, technology, eating habits, political regimes, knowledge, beliefs, rules and so on. We only need to consider the increasingly rapid succession of energy sources that humans have used throughout history. For millennia, they relied on their muscle force and the heat of fire; then, they domesticated a few animal species to harvest their strength – as well as that of slaves, who were not treated much better than those animals. Later, humans found a way to use the energy of the wind and water courses, and then they learned to use coal to fuel steam engines. From then on, the succession became faster and faster: coal was joined by oil, then methane, gas and, finally, nuclear fission, to return (hopefully) to renewable sources, such as wind and sunlight. As children, the grandparents and great-grandparents of our students warmed themselves with wood stoves, and now, at least in some countries, they use the electric energy produced by wind turbines, solar panels or nuclear plants. All this happened over one or two generations. We have seen this in the previous chapters, where we discussed acceleration. Acceleration is not only expressed through the increasingly frenetic rhythms of life in the age of hyper-modernity, it also impacts the relationships between generations.

As we noted, one obvious consequence of the acceleration of change is the fact that between the life and death of an individual, the world in which they live in is no longer the same. Furthermore, change impacts everything, from the most minute aspects of daily life to the processes of production and consumption, the rise and fall of the great powers who rule the world, and even climate change. The vast majority of the people who reach old age have lived through different historical periods over their lifetimes. We all live in the same time, but we are not contemporaries: the world changes, and humans adapt to change. Adaptation does not mean passive adjustment to external changes; it is also the ability to manage change according to one's life horizons. Adaptation is the price we have to pay to avoid feeling constantly asynchronized, neither early nor late, with what happens in the world. However, the ability of humans to adapt to change is very much variable, depending on their degree of rigidity or flexibility, or openness or closedness to the world around them. The factors influencing their ability to adapt are various and can involve an individual's personality traits and their relationship with the environment. One of the most important factors is undoubtedly the phase of life in which they are called to deal with change.

Conventional wisdom, as well as a huge amount of scientific literature, teaches us that childhood, adolescence and youth are the phases of maximum malleability of orientations, attitudes and behaviours, which will retain a degree of persistence in the later phases of life. The formative years are critical, though an individual's openness to change and learning can survive into their old age. The path is forged by the continual interaction of the forming subject with their close and distant environment, going, as Bronfenbrenner (1979) argues, from the micro- via the meso- to the macro-system. In other words, formation is the work not only of the family, school and peer group but also of everything that happens in the environment.

Thus, the generational approach is grounded on the hypothesis that experiencing a situation, an event or a sequence of historical events in the formative phase of the life course, produces a learning process that can engage a plurality of subjects. This hypothesis, which is supported by cognitive psychology studies, argues that the experience of an event produces learning: (1) if it crosses the threshold of the subject's selective perception and attention; (2) if it contrasts in some way with the available information as is organized in the mind, producing a sort of 'surprise effect'; and (3) if it causes a restructuring of the subject's cognitive maps, and, therefore, of their orientation systems and world images. We must keep in mind that individual cognitive maps are shared, or at least similar to one another on a cognitive level, so that the learning process is socially enforced by the fact that it is shared by other members of the peer group with which the subject interacts. The restructuring of cognitive maps is made easier to the extent that these maps are (as in the formation phase) still scarcely consolidated and are supported, validated and confirmed by the peer community.

A sort of generational collective memory is then formed through the cognitive and emotional elaboration of key events experienced by the subjects. This memory is composed of beliefs, opinions, symbols, myths and attributions of meaning, and is bound to remain relatively stable. Over the years, cognitive maps become less and less receptive, acting as a filter that excludes discording experiences and information that would challenge their integrity, and that only accepts those that confirm and strengthen their acquired beliefs and convictions. A very significant aspect of our way of approaching reality, both cognitively and emotionally, relates to what we can take for granted: if everything surprised us as if we were seeing it for the first time, we would be constantly bewildered by new stimuli, which would undercut the functioning of our mental faculties. What we can take for granted is what we learned as children, enriching it and accumulating it in later life phases. However, what we can take for granted is very much tied to the formative phases of life, and in an age of accelerated social change, it also changes from generation to generation: what was taken for granted by our grandparents was not as valid for our parents and is no longer valid for us.

In societies characterized by slow changes, whose rhythms encompassed several generations, there were no interruptions; as Helga Nowotny (2021) observed, when a community decided to build a cathedral at the centre of a town, they knew it would take many generations to complete it. The acceleration of change, on the other hand, creates discontinuity. To make just one very obvious example, we only need to think of the changes brought about by digital technologies and the different capacity of appropriation of this potential depending on the life stage in which we experienced the impact of these technologies. We rightly speak of 'digital natives' and of the inversion of the generational relationship when it comes to learning the use of these instruments: grandparents and parents have, in many cases, learned from their own children and grandchildren. This is even more true of those phenomena that, for their very nature (for instance, fashion), are subject to frequent and rapid change. One example among many we could cite is the practice of using tattoos to modify, more or less permanently, one's physical appearance. This practice has been adopted by the young, imitated by many middle-aged men and even women, but the older population has remained almost entirely excluded from it.

Therefore, the fact of living in the same historical time but having lived the formative years in different phases of historical-social development produces significant consequences for the relationship between generations. This is true of the relationships between parents and children, between students and teachers, and even between contiguous generations. While interacting with other people, we frequently realize that we speak different languages (even if only partially different). This makes communication difficult, and this difficulty is precisely what makes us aware of the fact that we belong to different generations. While historical-social change produces the phenomenon of generations, change itself is, in turn, made possible by generational metabolism. In any social group or organization, and in society at large, change can happen in two ways: through individual members – via mechanisms of re-socialization (pedagogic initiatives, campaigns of re-education and continuous training) that attempt to modify established attitudes and behaviours; or through the replacement of the members themselves, introducing new cohorts with different characteristics from the old ones and waiting for these to leave the scene. This second approach is much more effective given the limited pliability of individual behaviours after the formative stage. Social 'bodies' undergo a similar process to the one experienced by living organisms, in which the replacement of lower-level components (for example, the cells of an organ) ensures the capacity for change and adaptation of the whole organism.

Distance and closeness of generations within the family

A few decades ago, in the wake of the student and youth movements of the late 1960s and early 1970s, there was frequent talk of generational conflicts – both from those who entrusted them with their hopes for the future and from those who feared their disruptive effects. Today, this phenomenon seems to have vanished from reality, as well as from the attention of scholars. As we will see, it has reappeared in a different form in environmental movements – in which, however, the anagraphic/generational element is not the essential trait. However, we must recognize that there are objective conditions, especially economic ones, that would hypothetically be likely to produce generational conflict (Schizzerotto et al, 2011).

In general terms, we can affirm that the societies that have accumulated a large public debt show a tendency to satisfy their current needs at the expense of future generations. This also has to do with what has been called the presentification syndrome. The present (the today) tends to prevail on the future (the tomorrow). At an economic level, borrowing has a different temporal meaning if the credit is needed to finance investments or consumption. In the former case, it contributes to building the future; in the latter, it contributes to mortgage it. Saving, on the other hand, leads to the renunciation of the present in sight of possible uses at a later time, as in cases of emergency (cautious behaviour) or to reserve the saved resources to future investments. The rules of behaviour of traditional bourgeois families (though not only them) in the past followed the principle of delayed gratification. The protestant ethic illustrated by Max Weber imposes a sober life because what matters is the success of the enterprise rather than the immediate well-being of the entrepreneur's family. In the consumption society of the late-modern age, these rules have been suspended: for many, the ethos of saving has been replaced by the propensity for speculative investment, which promises profits in the short term.

From a macro perspective, the resort to public debt, particularly to finance current expenses, penalizes the future generations who will at one point have to pay the debt made by the previous generations, unless exogenous dynamics intervene (as happened with the world wars) to subvert or cancel it. Beyond public debt, in phases of public finances crisis, it is often easier, from a political consensus perspective, to reduce education expenses – penalizing the young – than it is to reduce the expenses allocated to retirement provisions for the older population. Pension expenditure is generally more rigid than the expenses for childhood, adolescence and youth, which is already decreasing because of the drop in birthrate. With the increase in the average age of the population, the quota of elders in the electorate is bound to keep growing, while the younger electorate will decrease. For the same reason, healthcare expenditure, as it is mostly destined to the elderly, is hardly reducible. This is potentially detrimental to preventive medicine, which could be more beneficial to young people. Despite these objective reasons for a conflict of interest at a macro-economic level, in this historical phase, a sense of pacific indifference seems to prevail in the relationships between generations (Woodman and Wyn, 2014).

Conflict signals the presence of a strong relationship between the parties. It appears that conflict has disappeared for a variety of reasons, but one of these is the acceleration that has increased the distance between the generations. This is true both when young people achieve a precocious autonomy from their families (as in the societies of Northern Europe) and when many young people live with their families for longer, continuing to take advantage of the benefits of dependence while enjoying significant autonomy in managing their own lifestyles (as is the case in Southern Europe). This physical closeness, however, does not erase the distance, and economic dependence does not necessarily mean submission to parental power. The family often plays a decisive role in the redistribution of resources among generations, for instance, grandparents' pensions sometimes help pay for their grandchildren's education or support them in their phases of unemployment. In this case, the underlying conflict is not expressed because the family acts as a cushion. To simplify, we can say that the parents' generation has understood that their sons and daughters speak a different language and are going to live in a different way from them, and that their task is guaranteeing their present and the necessary cultural and economic resources to face an uncertain future, on which they will not be able to have much influence and that, either way, will be rather unpredictable.

As for the interference and interdependence among the past, present and future, an important aspect of the relationship between generations revolves around the hereditary transmission of assets. Clearly, this only applies to families who have something – either positive or negative – to leave behind. Sometimes, less-than-provident parents leave unpaid debts to their descendants, for instance, a mortgage whose payments have not yet ended. With the diffusion of sub-prime loans, this is all but a rare instance, especially in the US and in the middle and lower-middle classes. However, when it comes to family assets, it is no coincidence that many parents anticipate their transmission to sons and daughters through donations, as otherwise, due to the prolongation of life, their heirs would receive them when they are already too old. Parents who can afford it tend to contribute fully or partially to the acquisition of an autonomous home for their children when they leave the family home. Especially in Southern European countries, the home has a high symbolic value, as it incorporates the idea of family continuity. Hereditary transmission has peculiar aspects based on the nature of the assets and eventual plurality of the heirs. Frequently, conflict emerges not between different generations but within the same generation, between first and second born, male and female, legitimate and illegitimate, and favoured and penalized children.

The casuistry is ample, as lawyers and judges specialized in succession law know. Even in funeral rites and in the care of the memory of the deceased, signs of continuity in the succession of generations are almost disappearing. Not only are family tombs increasingly rare but the diffusion of cremation itself strongly reduces the material symbol of such continuity, highlighting the growing distance between generations. We need not think, however, that the distance caused by the speed of change between generations in the family is always accompanied by emotional distance. There are parents and children who do not live in the same time and place but remain deeply close, often telephoning each other, exchanging messages and traveling to each other as much as they can to keep the bond alive. Family relationships transform, but family as an institution is still fundamental, despite its numerous metamorphoses. There has been much talk, often with apocalyptic tones, of family crisis. The frequency of divorces and separations, as well as cases of violence against women and minors, and mental pathologies that can be attributed to the malfunctioning of family relationships, seem to validate this pessimistic view. However, in reality, the crisis involves the traditional models of family based on rigid gender and age hierarchies, while family shows a remarkable capacity to adapt to the changes that, in some ways, it contributes to create. In fact, family appears to be quite resistant even to the growing distance between the generations it is made up of (Löckenhoff and Rutt, 2015).

Distance and closeness of generations in education

There is no doubt that the distance between generations has significant consequences for education processes as well. School, by definition, is an institution where different generations meet. This is especially true in those societies in which the average age of teachers is quite high. In some countries, high-school students normally have teachers who are 30 to 40 years older than them. In primary school, the age gap is even wider. In Europe, recruitment policies have led to very varied situations as to the age distribution of teachers: in Italy, at all levels of education, the quota of teachers under 30 is almost insignificant (only 2 per cent), while 58 per cent are older than 50. Older teachers were trained in another time, and they do not always manage to sympathize with the students and their culture, which is made more with pictures and less with words, and has found new forms of expression and language in social media. Faced with these relational difficulties, some teachers retreat to technical knowledge and the contents of their subjects, favouring the task of instruction over education.

One of the most obvious consequences of acceleration is that the future has become more and more uncertain and unpredictable. This had important consequences for the processes of intergenerational transmission, especially in the schools educating adolescents and youth. In the slow times of the past, the wisdom of the elders (who were few) was the asset to be handed down to new generations. Acceleration has eroded that capital of wisdom. Today, we need to train new generations to deal with a world when none of us know what it will be like. We need to provide them with the certainties that will enable them to face uncertainty. The risk of an uncertain future reducing the temporal horizon, favouring the erasure of the past and the shortening of the future, and causing a retreat to the present and the immediate dimension, is clearly real. School cannot fall short of its duty of transmitting knowledge and contributing to the elaboration of memory. However, beyond this task, education should also have a role of making young people confident that they can face the uncertainty of their collective and individual futures. Confidence in ourselves, in other humans and in the world is the great resource that empowers us to fight uncertainty: confidence in our abilities, but with an awareness of our limitations. This is a very difficult task, for which many teachers have not been trained. Many of them warn, often unwittingly, that acceleration has made many of their skills obsolete and that their distance from the culture of their students, who effectively live in a different time, has become difficult to bridge. School as an institution has a hard time defining its function in an ever-changing world. These difficulties are often expressed in the pedagogic discourse through the opposition of knowledge and skills. Clearly, school cannot stop transmitting knowledge and building skills; the problem arises when it is no longer clear how much of the transmitted knowledge should be preserved and which skills have become obsolete. Faced with these questions, teachers are polarized between innovation and conservation, and many of them have lost a clear understanding of the nature of their task. This explains why some teachers suffer from burnout syndrome. Since one of the main functions of education is to form individuals with a reasonable sense of trust in the world – and, more importantly, in themselves – the presence of a quota of depressed teachers is hardly encouraging. Moreover, in the advanced societies of the West, teachers do not enjoy much social prestige. On a subjective level, they perceive that this prestige has diminished over time, especially when they interact with the parents of their middle- and upper-middle-class students, who often look down on them and do not recognize their authority.

In pedagogic terms, as suggested by the modern science of education (Schleicher, 2018), school should encourage those who struggle more to fully develop their capacities and teach the talented not to underestimate challenges and to be aware of their limitations. When it comes to facing the future, confidence is the most important resource, and school is too often not a supportive environment for its development. On the one hand, school tends to discourage the category of 'underachievers' and reward 'overachievers', contributing to amplify the inequalities determined by the social backgrounds of their families of origin. We can wonder if school contributes to increase or reduce the distance between generations if it does more to preserve the past or to build the future of youths – who, one way or another, spend a significant portion of their time within its walls. The answer to this question depends on the structure of school systems, on their history, on the orientation of school policies, on the strategies of the users (families and youth) and – obviously – on the teachers' training. From this point of view, even if we only consider the Western world, we are faced with great variety. This is not the time for an even synthetic overview. However, it is important to reflect on the fact that all education systems are currently under the influence of contrasting tendencies, simultaneously pointing to conservation, or even restoration, and innovation; the tension between memory and future, which is the subject of this book, runs through the world of education, sometimes in a lacerating way. The ambivalence surrounding the future is reflected in teaching and particularly in teaching history, where the memory of the past seams to both teachers and students irrelevant to understanding the present and the future.

The category of teachers regularly incorporates deep and contradictory cultural currents. Their attitudes express the uncertainties that characterize our society. As we will see in more detail in the Conclusion of this book, even in the response to the pandemic, there were polarizations that reveal the ambivalence of future images typical of historical periods that experience processes of abrupt change. At least since the end of the 17th century, there have been disputes between ancient and modern values. Since then, social and political thinking has swung between the prophets of progress and others who express nostalgia for the past, pointing at signs of decline and decadence, and even predicting catastrophes and doom – two currents, with all their variants, looking at both the past and the future, but with different eyes and opposed perspectives. Often, though not always, these visions intertwine with the culture being transmitted by teachers at school without any effort towards the synthesis, integration or even critical analysis of reasons and differences.

The opposition between the ideas of progress and decadence has run the length of the intellectual history of the 1800s and 1900s. In 1920, John Bury, a Cambridge historian, dedicated a svelte and successful volume titled *The Idea of Progress* (Bury, 2023 [1920]) to the memory of the Abbée de Saint Pierre, Condorcet, Comte and Spencer, 'and other optimists mentioned in this book'. In those same years, another book was published in Germany, *Der Untergang des Abendlandes* (*The Decline of the West*) by Oswald Spengler (1962 [1918]), which, in a way, condenses the opposite view, according to which Western civilization is inevitably doomed to decline. From the Enlightenment to Spengler, stopping by Nietzsche, historical and philosophical thinking oscillated between these two poles. At the end of the 1950s, the issue was revisited in a different key when Charles Percy Snow (1959) wrote a famous booklet to signal the divergence between the culture of scientists and the culture of intellectuals: the former generally optimistic about the possibilities opened by technological and scientific progress, the latter generally pessimistic about the loss of the values inherited from the classic and humanistic ages. A few years later, in 1964, Umberto Eco published *Apocalittici e Integrati*, where he described the opposition between the aristocratic cultural pessimism of those who criticized mass culture and those who exalted its democratic virtues (see Eco, 2000). Snow and Eco are only two of the many examples we could quote to illustrate a tension that takes many different, and often contradicting, forms, sometimes in very diverse realms of contemporary culture (Schiavone, 2022).

The problem for young men and women does not merely come from being exposed – through their parents and most of all through their teachers – to often-conflicting messages; it also comes from not having been trained to navigate a contradictory world in which choice is often difficult. When this exposure to opposing messages is not mediated by a critical ability to evaluate them, it can cause confusion and retreat into the peer group, where they feel protected among people who experience the same situation as them, but where isolation and distance from the adults' generations grow. This picture, while it highlights a difficulty in choosing, does not imply that, most of the time, a choice is not eventually made. However, these choices are often quite precarious and reversible, and prefigure non-linear paths to adult life.

The difficulties we alluded to are also related to the different uses young people and adults make of the communication tools of the digital era. If the generations of the 19th century had witnessed the spread of printed media and newspapers, and the generations of the 20th century had listened to the radio and watched television, the generations of the 21st century communicate through social media. No communication tool replaces and erases the ones that came before it, but their weight and centrality evidently vary according to the age of their users. We rarely see a young person holding a newspaper or carrying a book; rather, we are much more likely to see them staring at their mobile phones. This different exposure to various communication means has an impact on thinking habits and the constitution of the public sphere. Opinions are formed through the sharing, and sometimes clashing, of different ideas, interpretations and world views. Citizens have always selected the communication channels that enable them to confirm and strengthen their personal ideas: whenever possible, a conservative citizen will choose circles of people who more or less share their likes and read the same newspapers read by them, and the same applies to citizens with progressive tendencies. Those who want to understand before choosing their allegiance will try to broaden their sources in order to make a more informed choice. The same goes for the television station they will go to for information and opinions, though in this case, there is a higher chance of being exposed to opinions opposing each other in less-than-civil ways. Young people read newspapers much less frequently, are less attracted by the television screen and are much more present online. Studies carried out throughout the Western world inform us that their presence on Facebook is rather limited (though more than proportional compared to other age groups), while Twitter and Instagram have a predominantly young user base. The difference, compared to traditional media, is that on social media, thanks to the 'molecular' connection mechanisms established by the algorithms, the probability to encounter different opinions is dramatically reduced, and, indeed, the explanation of these mechanisms often relies on the 'contagion' metaphor. Despite the volume of international research on this issue, we cannot yet say what the effects will be on the processes of formation of public opinion. What is certain is that, at least at this stage, this is another factor contributing to create distance between the generations.

Political generations: discontinuities, conflicts, silences and removals

We are contemporaries, as we said, but we belong to different historical phases. The first to use the concept of generations in this perspective was, notoriously, Karl Mannheim. Mannheim (1952 [1928]) developed his concept of generations as analogous to the concept of 'class situation': as the class situation unites and influences (but does not determine) individual destinies, so does generational collocation unite the individuals belonging to contiguous cohorts within the same historical-social context that influences their way of feeling, thinking and acting, providing a potential base for collective action. However, exposure to the same historical context – also known as '*Generationslagerung*' ('generational collocation') – is not sufficient to characterize a generation: not all people of the same age belong to the same generation (some are cut off from the course of events because they do not take part, not even indirectly or by reflection, in what happens on the historical scene). A *Generationszusammenhang* ('generational link'), that is, a common orientation to the current historical context, is necessarily established between those who are exposed to the same generational situation.

The contents of such an orientation, however, are not necessarily identical or uniform; rather, they vary with belonging to different 'generational units'. The groups that form within these units are the true depositaries of the generational units themselves (here, Mannheim is referring, above all, to the groups that were part of the so-called '*Jugendbewegung*' in early 1900s' Germany, a youth movement that looked to nature as the authentic source of life as opposed to the artificiality of bourgeois life). The plurality of generational units reflects the articulation and the social fractures emerging from other dimensions (for instance, class structure produces as many generational units as there are main classes).

A generational situation does not automatically translate to a 'generational link'; the latter emerges only when the acceleration of the historical-social dynamic no longer allows for the simple hereditary transmission of the traditional ways of feeling, thinking and acting. A critical influence in this sense is determined by the events resulting from collective mobilization, which act as crystallization points, or as 'generational entelechies' reflecting the *zeitgeist* of a given age and the different ways to interpret it. As Mannheim (1952 [1928]: 297) writes:

> the fact that people are born at the same time, or that their youth, adulthood and old age coincide, does not in itself involve similarity of location; what does create a similar location is that they are in a position to experience the same events … and especially that these experiences impinge upon a similarly 'stratified' consciousness … mere chronological contemporaneity cannot in itself produce a common generation location.

Mannheim maintains that individual consciousness is composed of several strata, the deepest of which is impressed with the first experiences that delineate the framework in which successive experiences are placed and assigned meaning. Adults and elders live in a preformed world, so to speak, in which every new experience finds its own form and collocation, which is predetermined by the sedimentation of previous experiences, while for young people, the situations in which they live their first experiences shape and mould the basic structures of their consciousness.

Mannheim does not specify the modalities in which the events individuals are exposed to in their phase of maximum malleability intervene in the formation of the cognitive and emotional structures of individual personality. In order to leave a lasting mark on an entire generation, early experiences must be able to engage a sufficient number of people in a non-superficial way: they must be able, as Durkheim would say, to create collective emotions or enthusiasms in those who participate in them. Mannheim reflected on the way in which the vicissitudes of German society between the 19th and 20th centuries – from the formation of the Reich via the First World War to the Republic of Weimar – had marked profound differences between the generations, differences that he observed first hand. The conceptual framework proposed by Mannheim was then freely applied to study generational phenomena in other historical-political contexts. Wars, as well as abrupt social changes, heavily influence the formation of generational fractures. In Germany, as we saw in Chapter One, youth movements between the late 1960s and the early 1970s revealed deep conflicts with the generation of their parents and grandparents, who had more or less supported National Socialism.

In the US, the Vietnam War left a deep mark on the experiences of the young generations involved. The rapid and massive transformations witnessed by Eastern European societies before and after the fall of the Berlin Wall and the dissolution of the Soviet Union have also caused deep generational fractures (Cavalli, 2020). It was a crucial event, with far-reaching social implications, which left traces in individual biographies – a concept reiterated by Heberle (1951: 122), who called it a 'decisive and politically relevant experience'. Even the movements that fall under the label of the 'Arab Spring', which developed mostly in North African and Middle Eastern societies, had a clear generational character. As we hinted, there was a historical period roughly half a century ago in which generational conflict was a much debated and studied issue, at least in the Western world. Youth movements were seen as manifest forms of opposition of sons and daughters to mothers and fathers, both at a familial and at a societal level. However, even though the protagonists of these movements were for the most part youths, we cannot call this a true generational conflict; rather, it was actually a historically localized phenomenon at the end of a phase of extraordinary economic and social development that involved the whole West after the Second World War. This period has been called the 'glorious thirty years' (Crafts and Toniolo, 1996): a (probably unrepeatable) time of outstanding economic growth, coupled with an unprecedented quantitative expansion of higher education systems that radically transformed the social composition of the student population. Periods of such intense change breed the conviction that not only do societies change, but they can also be changed, modified and shaped by the intentional and collective action of social movements of reform, or even revolutionary movements. In other words, great and rapid social transformations such as the ones that happened in that historical phase create conditions that favour the emergence of social movements, which, in turn, cause further transformations (Tarrow, 1989; Della Porta and Diani, 2020).

Intergenerational transmission – from parents to children, from grandparents to grandchildren and from teacher to students – does not always happen without friction: sometimes, there are fractures and interruptions; sometimes, it happens partially or in a deformed or distorted way. When transmission is interrupted or disturbed, this is a sign of the likely presence of processes of removal. As we have seen, this was the case in Germany with the memory of Nazism and in Italy with the memory of fascism and the *Resistenza* (Cavalli, 2013). In the 20 years of post-war reconstructions, the fascist period was removed from public consciousness and replaced by the myth/monument of the resistance. The *Resistenza* was indeed a movement of active minorities with deep popular roots, especially in the northern regions of the country – a movement that gave moral redemption to the country after the traumatic experience of the regime. However, the *Resistenza* has also contributed to validate the thesis that fascism was a dark parenthesis lacking deeper popular roots and elements of continuities in the history of the Italian state. It has contributed to conceal its deep territorial fractures and, last but not least, to understate the decisive role of allied armies in freeing Europe and Italy from fascism and the German occupation. Only later, in more recent years, has historical research, thanks to the studies by De Felice, Gentile, Pavone and others, begun to erode the foundations of this removal process – which, however, has not yet penetrated many deeper layers of public opinion. Similar processes have certainly developed in Spain,

Greece, Portugal and, later, Russia and Eastern Europe, that is, in all the cases of change in which a political regime that did not lack popular consensus was replaced by a successive regime that grounded its legitimacy on underlining their discontinuity. Removal inevitably interrupts communication between generations, and later generations are not always able to repair the fracture. We could cite many other historical examples in this regard.

The relationships between generations in the era of COVID-19, the return of war and the environmental crisis

We have seen how the acceleration of the rhythm of change, which implys a variety of aspects of individual and social life, has had an impact on relationships within the family, the school and the public sphere between subjects belonging to different generations. Now, we need to focus on a series of events that shaped our recent past and, most of all, will shape the immediate future: the COVID-19 pandemic, the reappearance of war in Europe and climate change – and, more generally, the environmental crisis, which is a watershed in the historical development of human societies and will clearly affect the relationship between generations.

Starting with the most recent event, there is no doubt that the reappearance of war in the heart of Europe with the invasion of Ukraine by Putin's Russia marks a historical turning point. After the Second World War, Europe has lived one of the longest periods of peace in its history. It is true that France and other former colonial states have been engaged in wars of independence in their former colonies. It is true that there had been tanks in Budapest and Prague, as well as echoes of the Korea and Vietnam wars. It is also true that war in the Balkans caused tremendous bloodshed and destruction. However, it was the war in Ukraine that suddenly awakened European society to the possibility of direct involvement in its own homeland. This is clearly the case for the populations of the states involved in the conflict, who had to start counting their losses, both civilian and military, but even the case for those who witness the conflict from the outside, supplying arms, receiving refugees and fearing its possible extension. In much of Europe, only less than 5 per cent of the population has personal memories of war from when they were children. Everyone else may have studied history, read books, watched films and perhaps listened to their parents' and grandparents' stories. As we know, those who experienced and survived a war often did not want to share this experience for several years, telling stories about what they had seen. Memory of the war has not completely vanished from European consciousness, but it has certainly faded. Remote memories may have resurfaced in old people, but young people may only have the virtual dimension of war games as reference, which could be consoling and worrying at the same time.

Supposing that humanity might have developed something like a collective consciousness, this is certainly tied to the risk of a nuclear war. The Second World War ended with the use, for the first time, of atomic bombs on the cities of Hiroshima and Nagasaki. After the end of the war, for several decades, the bipolar system of the Cold War prevented the nuclear confrontation that would have destroyed the two superpowers and the rest of the world with them. We can say that the proliferation of nuclear weapons in the hands of the two superpowers has prevented their use. Not trusting one another, each of them accumulated a destructive force that could convey the message that whoever dared to use that power would anyway be annihilated shortly after. At that time, humanity matured the awareness that it possessed the technical means for its own self-destruction. Today, the roughly 13,000 nuclear warheads possessed by a handful of big, medium and small powers have (hopefully) the only purpose of threatening their possible use so that everyone abstains from it. However, this threat would be ineffective if the risk of its enactment were totally and categorically ruled out. The human species lives in the awareness that it is capable of destroying itself.

However, the nuclear threat is not the only danger facing humanity. While this depends on the decisions of the leaders of the states that possess atomic weapons, the COVID-19 pandemic, which has spread with great rapidity all around the world since the winter of 2019/20, has proven that even nature can threaten, almost simultaneously, all the human beings who live on Earth. The intensity and frequency of international relations do not, or only very partially, allow us to limit the contagion. The pandemic has clearly shown us not only the need for a coordinated worldwide response but also the difficulties in implementing it. The use of vaccines seems effective in reducing the effects of the virus, but we know that without a generalized vaccination of everyone in all continents, the virus can continuously mutate, threatening the health of our species.

The pandemic certainly had a much different impact depending on individuals' stage in the life cycle: less for its clinical and sanitary aspects, as well as the incidence of mortality, and much more for the disruption caused by the long lockdowns on relational life – in families and among peers – and on the regular functioning of the education system (Deeker, 2022). There is no doubt that the highest price was payed by elderly people who died, but also by the generations still engaged in formative processes. This phenomenon, however, has a different meaning from the events we just recalled because it involved, unexpectedly and almost simultaneously, all the societies of the planet and the relationship between the species *homo sapiens* and nature's reaction to the modifications caused by its (intrusive) presence.

COVID-19 has made us suddenly realize that we are all on the same ship – something we should have learned at least half a century ago. In 1972, Massachusetts Institute of Technology (MIT) researchers Donella and Dennis Meadows had already warned that our planet's resources are not unlimited and, therefore, unlimited growth is unthinkable (Meadows et al, 1972). In 1990, the first report of the Intergovernmental Panel on Climate Change (IPCC) signalled the risks of global warming caused by the accumulation of carbon dioxide and other gasses in the atmosphere. Later, the United Nations Framework Convention on Climate Change's Kyoto Protocol on 11 December 1997, Paris Agreement on 12 December 2015 and, finally, Glasgow Climate Pact on 13 December 2021 were the most significant events marking the development of public awareness about the dangers faced by humanity.

We cannot identify any specific culprits for the risk situation that has emerged over the last two-and-a-half centuries, though especially over the last 50 years. Climate change is a consequence of the industrial phase of human history, when, at the end of the 18th century, humans began using fossil fuels to produce the energy previously derived only from fire, wind and the muscle power of humans and animals. This triggered a cumulative process, first in Europe, then in North America and Japan, and over the last 30 years in India, China and some areas of Latin America.

The scientists who study climate change seem to agree on the fact that unless we reduce to zero the emissions of carbon dioxide and other greenhouse gasses into the atmosphere by 2050, so that the average temperature on the planet does not exceed 1.5°C above pre-industrial levels, the damages to the environment will be permanent and could, in the long run, even threaten the survival of our species. When this could happen is largely unpredictable, but we do know that if, as a species, we do nothing in the next 30 years, the outcome of the process towards the uninhabitability of our planet could rapidly get closer. In 30 years, those who are being born today will be at the onset of adulthood. Others will be in the middle of their existences, and those who are old today will for the most part already be dead. To different extents and in different forms, the environmental challenge involves all dwellers of the Earth: rich or poor, living in the Global North or South, and women and men of all ages (Chakrabarty, 2021). However, it also creates deep inequalities, as it hits entire populations that, both in the past and in the present, have contributed nothing or very little to global warming. In the so-called 'advanced societies', awareness is growing that the model of development that carried them all into the present is not feasible for the other populations that are only now joining, or have only recently joined, what we have gotten used to calling 'modernity'.

Limiting our reflection to the so-called 'Western societies', we ask: what is the attitude of the various generations regarding the environmental challenge? Synthesizing some findings from the literature on this topic, we can identify seven types of attitude (Dechezleprêtre, 2022; Wray, 2022):

- Obviously, there are people who do not concern themselves with this issue because they are too busy trying to secure their own day-by-day survival. This is the portion of people who are below or very close to the poverty line. For the poor, the risk of climate change is too far from their daily preoccupations, unless directly hit by some extreme weather phenomenon. This goes for young people as well as adults and elders.
- Then, there are those who are either effectively shielded from public communication or have never paused to reflect on the implications of climate change because, either way, their temporal horizon is short. We can imagine that in our societies, those who are still relatively ignorant about the environmental risk are a minority, in which the youth quota is however small.
- Another attitude includes those who have been touched by the information regarding the environmental crisis but have removed the problem, either consciously or unconsciously. This operation of removal is driven by a vague sense of danger, however remote, which they are unwilling to recognize. I would put forward the hypothesis that, in this

case, there may be a higher percentage of adults and elders and a lower percentage of young people.

- Then, there are those who distance the problem by adhering to denialist theories. Although there is now high consensus among climate experts that these changes are in great part determined by the impact of human activity, there is still a slim minority who claims that the alternation between periods of warming and cooling of the Earth is unrelated to human action but depends on geophysical and astronomical factors. There is no doubt that a significant portion of our societies hides behind the dissenting scientists' opinion to avoid facing the problem. Research carried out in various countries tells us that young people are much less receptive to denialist theories compared to the adult and elder population.
- Some people take the presence of environmental risk so seriously that they are terrified by the possible consequences for the inhabitability of the planet and are overtaken by a catastrophizing syndrome that feeds a real future anxiety. Feelings and emotions of this sort are common among young people, though not limited to them. Sometimes, young couples come to the decision of not generating children to spare them the suffering of living in a decaying world. Some scholars have hypothesized that this could be a significant factor behind the demographic decline in many parts of the world (Vignoli et al, 2022).
- On the opposite side, that is, positive views of the future, we find those who take the risks related to climate change seriously but have faith in the possibility that human societies, aided by scientific and technological progress, might reverse these processes and recreate conditions of habitability, not only for humans but also for all the other forms of animal and plant life. This is the attitude of younger and less young people who have faith in science, in the development of alternative energy sources, in the possibility to remove excess carbon dioxide from the atmosphere and

reintroduce it in the depths of the Earth, and in the ability of human societies to develop activities and lifestyles that are more respectful of the natural environment.

- Finally, one last type comprises those who perceive the threat to our species as extremely serious but feel compelled to intervene to avert the worst and mobilize to push global elites to make the necessary decisions to avoid the nefarious consequences of inaction. We are obviously referring to the movements (primarily youth movements) that have emerged in the last decade all over the world calling for a decisive change of course in environmental, economic and social policy, as well as a non-predatory relationship between society and nature. The reference to Friday for Future, a movement that has spread in numerous countries since 2018, is obvious. However, we are also thinking of the 'green' movements and parties that have occupied, with changing fortunes, the political scene of many countries over the last 50 years.

The quality of the groups exhibiting these various attitudes varies significantly in space and time. One of the main factors influencing their outcomes and their distribution is the degree of vulnerability to extreme events related to climate change, in particular, exposure to: prolonged periods of high temperatures; phases of extreme drought that compromise crops; the desertification of once-fertile areas; wildfires that destroy large forest areas; glacier retreat and raising sea levels; the devastating violence of tropical cyclones; landslides and rockfalls in mountain areas; and the extinction of animal and plant species that fail to adapt to sudden, or even gradual, climate change.

Exposure to frequent and serious events attributable to global warming has the effect of reducing indifference, as it becomes increasingly less credible to deny the evidence that we are faced with a global danger. On the other hand, cognitive and emotional proximity to extreme climate situations contributes to strengthen the last three attitudes we just examined: climate anxiety; trust in science and in the possibility to adopt the measures it suggests; and the mobilization impulse. The immediate experience of danger and the consequences of the mental and material damage suffered, however, can also feed a feeling of despair and prompt the fleeing of impacted areas. However, these three attitudes can generate a positive interaction, strengthening one another: climate anxiety can stimulate an active approach, a desire to join others who share the same concerns and confidence in the possibility that collective action may act as a pressure group and influence the decision processes of policy makers. Moreover, research conducted in communities that have been hit hard by events attributable to climate change has highlighted how responses that can mobilize solidarity and a civic sense significantly reduce post-traumatic stress disorder (PTSD) and facilitate recovery processes (Berry et al, 2010).

This virtuous synergy, however, requires a certain degree of convergence of temporal horizons. In a strictly individualistic perspective, the temporal horizon does not exceed personal life expectancies: it is necessarily short for people who passed a certain age, longer for middle-aged people and much longer for young people, who have much more future ahead of them. In a familistic perspective, temporal horizons embrace, in addition to one's own life, the lives of children and grandchildren, with an eye to family continuity. Traditional aristocracies also used to think beyond the time of the closest generations because they considered the traditions and the future of their lineage. In our present societies, if we symbolically consider an average family composed of three generations (grandparents, children and grandchildren), its temporal horizon roughly encompasses a century: a long-enough time for the climate crisis to acquire subjective relevance and therefore dispose openness to action. Then, there are those who identify with collectivities that transcend individual existence, such as local communities, what could have been the fatherland or the nation in the past, and now even all of humanity. These people, whatever their age, feel a duty to face the environmental problem because they feel responsible for future generations, for the grandchildren of the grandchildren of their grandchildren, and for everyone who will be born on Earth. It is at this point, when the temporal horizon of responsibility extends to the far future, that the conditions emerge for an alliance between the two idle classes of contemporary modernity: young people who have most of their lives ahead and old people who have most of their lives behind.

Conclusion

This book was written, and published, at a very delicate stage in world history: in the wake of the COVID-19 emergency, which has revealed the vulnerability of all human societies when affected by viruses that know no boundaries; when war has returned to the heart of Europe, putting the global economy and world order under strain; and while facing the prospect of a worsening environmental crisis. Given the uncertainty of the global and local contexts, some focus their expectations and goals on the present. A kind of 'carpe diem' attitude seems to resurface, over and over again: from Horace via Lorenzo the Magnificent to *Dead Poet's Society*, that is, almost to the present day. Acceleration, one of the *leitmotifs* that run throughout all the analyses presented here, has probably contributed to accentuating this syndrome of presentism that seems to crush the past and narrow down our vision of the future.

However, as we have seen in the previous chapters, presentism is not the only key to understanding the spirit of our times, nor is it the most important one. Memory and the past do not vanish, regardless of whether one seeks to nostalgically propose them again in a future moment or draw on them to build this future. There is no future without a past, and there is no past if we ignore where we come from, where we are at present, and where we want to go. However, there is something new in the times we inhabit that was not present in past eras.

Over the past two centuries, palaeontologists have collected, classified, and catalogued fossil specimens to understand the succession of plant and animal life forms on Earth, a process that took millions of years. It is estimated that the species to which the human beings now living on Earth belong appeared relatively recently: about two hundred thousand years ago.

Many species have disappeared or become extinct, either because they were defeated in the struggle for survival by more adapted species or as a result of exogenous changes in environmental conditions. Although these facts can be found in books and we may even have studied them at school, they have only recently entered the collective consciousness of at least a part of humanity. Like many other species, the human species may one day become extinct; its presence on the planet is therefore only temporary.

As we have already noted, the event that triggered this awareness was the explosion of the first atomic bomb, which demonstrated the technical possibility of self-extinction. The environmental crisis is a further element that strengthens this awareness and a great opportunity to reconsider, from a new perspective, the great issues of the future, not only for that part of the world we inhabit but also for the rest of humanity that lives, and will one day live, on this planet. First of all, it encourages us to revisit – as we have seen in the previous chapters – the debate on modernity and post-modernity. As unstable as the concept of the West may be, we could argue that the idea of modernity was born in the West on the impetus of the revolutions that, ever since the 17th century, have affected science, political and economic institutions, and culture in all their aspects. Modernity, especially in terms of its economic value, was also grafted onto cultures outside the West, giving rise to multiple forms of 'modern' societies (Eisenstadt, 2000) that constitute variants,though without losing their matrix of origin. However, despite their diversity, they can no longer foreshadow the arrival point for those who have not yet, or only in part, embarked on the road towards modernity. No matter what we want to call it, the Western world has – successfully or not – spread a model of civilization, partially as a result of colonial domination and the exploitation of other continents, and this model is based on the massive use of natural resources, mass production, the mass consumption of goods and services (which is based on growth, understood essentially as the growth of a country's gross national product, and more or less democratic institutions). While some countries have taken the path of mass production and consumption, but not always adopted democratic institutions (for example, Russia and China), others – like India or Brazil – try to pass for something akin to a democracy.

With the onset of the environmental crisis, it is easy to imagine that the same model cannot be exported and generalized. Those who have not yet adopted it must pursue other avenues, developing less energy-consuming and more environmentally friendly solutions in particular, while those who have adopted it – recently or further in the past – must seek new routes. For several years now, scholars have been talking about 'de-growth' (Latouche, 2010 [2007]; Block, 2018; Jackson, 2021), wondering whether the capitalist system can be reconsidered from a perspective that has abandoned the objective of unlimited growth. The debate is, and will remain, open for a long time. Thus far, contradictions and conflicts arising from the explosion of inequality have been defused by the increase in resources made available and redistributed by growth. But will it be possible to ensure social cohesion in the face of the current, predictable increase in inequalities in each country without growth, and without redefining its terms? How will we manage crises in those areas of the world where the environment has suffered the greatest damage, without the respective societies having contributed to it in any way? And how will the lifestyles and consumption patterns change in those parts of the world that have historically been most responsible for the disastrous effects of pollution on the climate? In particular, we will have to consider the fate of the rapidly growing populations of the African continent, who rightly aspire to enjoy some of the benefits of our civilization but must not, and cannot, follow our model to achieve these. To move forward, we must change direction and make an effort – under the real pressure of the crisis – to design alternative futures. We must reopen spaces to think about possible futures. In this exercise of imagination, the traditional categories of left versus right, or conservative versus progressive, are not always entirely satisfactory. It is no coincidence that the environmental – or *green* – movements themselves are not easily inscribed under these labels. Likewise, responses to the pandemic crisis have led to an acceleration of the pace of work and life in the most affected sectors, while in others, it has favoured deceleration, allowing us to recover spaces and times that turbo-charged modernity had relegated to a distant past (Torres and Gros, 2022).

Given the highly interdependent nature of our contemporary societies, it is clear that individual states – even those of continental dimensions – can no longer effectively and individually address the major issues of peace and war, health, and the environment. Interdependence means that what happens in the farthest corner of the Earth will sooner or later produce direct and, more often than not, indirect effects in the rest of the world. The best-known and most recent of these effects is the rise of the information society, which was made possible by the Internet; a piece of information can thus be transmitted in real time, by satellite, from the most remote village in Siberia via Cape Town to the Tierra del Fuego and vice versa, whereas anyone with access to a mobile phone can potentially be connected to anybody else. Unless conflicts between world powers move into space and destroy most of the nearly five thousand artificial satellites that relentlessly orbit around the planet, this is an irreversible fact. The social organization of time is articulated at different levels: from the individual to the collective, and from the local to the global (Flaherty et al, 2020). For a little more than half a century, intercontinental flights have created the need to coordinate time globally, and thanks to the Internet, a global time now regulates and synchronizes a continuously growing number of human activities.

Furthermore, without the Internet, there would be little room for an international market that allows financial capital to cross (largely undisturbed) the borders of states and even the political regimes that govern these. In the process of economic globalization, the financial market has developed most rapidly and intensely, creating an unprecedented form of capitalism that is only remotely related to industrial capitalism, the latter being connected more to the production of goods and services for the market. Even the very curious and somewhat-disturbing phenomenon of cryptocurrencies is part of the unrestrained financing of an economy that has completely distanced itself from state guarantees and control. Another obvious consequence of globalization is the spectacular development of international trade, which intensified considerably after the fall of the Berlin Wall and China's entry into the world market. Interdependence must be understood as more than the mere exchange of finished goods that end up in the consumers' hands; at least half of world trade is attributable to intermediate products, which therefore constitute segments of international value chains.

Not only do information, capital, goods, and services move, but so too do women and men. Over the past 40 years, the global immigrant population (that is, people living in a country other than their country of birth) has almost tripled, reaching nearly three hundred million people; in Europe, immigrants amount to some 5 per cent of the population. It goes without saying that information and money travel more easily and rapidly than goods and human beings, but even the latter have started to move more and more, often as a result of wars or famine brought about by the devastating effects of climate crises.

Increased interdependencies take sovereignty away from states, as they give rise to needs and problems that can only be addressed and solved globally. Many aspects of the crisis of politics are due precisely to the inability to tackle a variety of problems; centres of political power have lost – to a greater or lesser extent as the case may be – the capacity to determine the factors on which the health, welfare, and future of their citizens depend. Indeed, when confronted with the radical nature of the challenges posed by globalization, the crisis of politics currently seems to be encouraging tendencies that point to the reversibility of the process, to opening up prospects for restoration, and to returning to the logics and practices of a nostalgically evoked world.

The terms 'de-globalization' and 'anti-globalism' frequently emerge, and there have undoubtedly been cyclical waves of globalization and de-globalization in history, with long-distance traffic routes opening and closing from time to time. This time, though, the watchword of 'de-globalization' is accompanied by the revival of sovereignism, nationalism, populism, and even denialism, which fails to acknowledge the anthropic origin of the climate crisis. In these conditions, the time horizons are not only short-range but also medium- and long-range: short-range, because we must begin to act now; medium- and long-range, because only future generations will be able to see the results. Without a planning logic that embraces all these temporal dimensions, it would be like giving up any degree of control over one's collective future.

The world seems to be facing a turning point where two different time horizons, or paths, open up: two paths, of which one enables us to look to the future with not only fear but also confidence, while the other prefers to resort to a past relived as myth. It is not a matter of retrieving the ideologies that once allowed us to foreshadow a future, albeit a distant one, in which it was possible to achieve – through the succession of generations – the utopia of a better and more just world. Nowadays, these visions of the future are the prerogative of optimists who still believe in progress and the radiant destinies of humanity, as well as of those who, looking at a still-distant future, visualize themselves on the edge of the abyss (the *Abgrund* of which Adorno spoke) in one of the many variants of contemporary environmental catastrophism. It is a question of acting in the present while thinking of the future, but without losing the memory of the past and being conscious of the risks that humanity is running. Moreover, the great moments of crisis in history were marked not only by the disintegration and collapse of orders, institutions, and empires, but, at the same time, by innovation and the construction of new possible futures. After all, revolutions never happen in ordinary times.

Most human beings are focused on their daily survival and do not look to the past and future beyond their time on Earth. Even the worship of the dead is no longer practised widely; hardly anyone still visits cemeteries, where a sovereign silence reigns, except on the annual Day of the Dead. '*Après moi le déluge*' ('After me, the flood deluge'), Louis XV allegedly said, but the phrase also fits the presentism of our current times. At this point, though, a moral problem arises. Are we to stop thinking beyond the private horizon of our own lives and those of our children and grandchildren? Are we to somehow feel responsible for those who have not yet been born and who will be born – our grandchildren, our grandchildren's grandchildren, and so on? This calls to mind the question raised by Hans Jonas in 1979, about the principle of responsibility, that is, whether we should allow humanity to engage in a slow collective suicide whose main victims will come after us.

The environmental crisis forces us to think realistically about a future that is not immediate but long-term; we must not only try to predict – as accurately as possible – what may happen in the future but also intervene, implementing actions and strategies whose effects will only become visible after some time, even a long time. To do so, we need people with a broad time horizon, who are capable of collective action. Seen from a long-term perspective, it is difficult to mobilize interests that require if not immediate, then at least short- to medium-term outcomes. For example, experts claim that nuclear fusion as a source of clean energy requires some 20 years of research and experimentation, and then another ten years for implementation, provided that the research and experiments yield positive results. But what private enterprise will be willing to invest large sums in a venture that may, or may not, provide profits only after 30 years? The situation is not very different in the public sphere, as even a government decision-maker – at least in a democratic regime – generally hesitates to embark on initiatives beyond the time horizon of election deadlines; it is no easy task to convince the electorate that we must operate in the present for the benefit of the generation of our grandchildren's grandchildren. Climate change, then, calls for a radical temporal reorientation. We must reflect on the actions to be taken today, tomorrow, and the day after tomorrow, in a long and coordinated time sequence, to avoid a catastrophe that is announced yet remote. Fear is an emotion that triggers immediate reactions of inaction (that is, when one remains helpless and paralyzed), flight, or aggression. From a biological evolution perspective, present-day human beings are not very different from the hunter-gatherers of a few tens of thousands of years ago: our predecessors had to react immediately to sudden and impending threats coming from the environment in which they lived; we have to react to deferred fears. The type of fear – assuming one can still call it such – that concerns climate change is very often a 'delayed' fear, except when one falls victim to an unexpected, extreme weather phenomenon. Hence, we must begin to act now to avoid an irreversible, short-term process of self-destruction of the species and its environment. The horizon of the present forces us to look not only far ahead but also to the near future.

Yet, precisely because preventive measures must be taken globally and with the cooperation of all states for the actions to be effective, the problem arises of whether to start the construction of a world order that, while respecting differences, guarantees a high degree of synergy and cooperation among peoples. This is the task of movements belonging to what Mary Kaldor (2003) calls 'global civil society'. A broad range of 'realist' thinkers will inevitably take it upon themselves to declare such a goal utopian, hence unattainable. 'Realist' thought is important because it warns us of the difficulties – of which we must be responsibly aware – when taking concrete actions in view of a distant goal. Nevertheless, we must not forget that the call for realism is often invoked by those who would like to leave things as they are, without venturing into the planning of possible futures.

Perhaps we must rethink, once again, the very meaning of the word 'utopia'. Utopia is a desirable – and therefore ideal – condition that concerns the future for which it makes sense to seriously start taking action in the present, even though its realization may take place far beyond our lifetime. This conception of utopia is different from the classical notion as developed by Thomas More, Campanella, and others. It is not a matter of designing an ideal island-city but of distinguishing a direction that promises to improve the human condition or at least ensure its continuation. What underlies utopian thought is a philosophy of history (albeit in a weak version, compared to 19th- and 20th-century philosophies), namely, the idea that historical development is directed towards a desirable, not necessary but possible, outcome and that it therefore still makes sense to strive for its achievement. Another element that underlies the great currents of thought – often wrongly called 'ideologies' – that have marked the last three centuries of history, from liberalism to socialism, was a philosophy of history that glimpsed the possibility of affirming the values of freedom and equality. The pursuit of the values of freedom and equality has been marked by multiple, often contradictory, historical paths (Cerutti, 2007). Not only have liberty and equality fuelled quite bitter struggles between currents of thought and social movements, as if liberalism and socialism were two opposing world views, but mutually incompatible trends have also developed within the respective camps. Think of the divide in liberal thought between neoliberalism, which exalts the role of the market and minimizes that of the state, and liberalism, which claims an active role for the state to correct market failures; otherwise, in the socialist camp, think of the dilemma between social democracy and communist statism, which has had dramatic consequences in the recent history of a large part of Europe (Felice, 2022).

The values of freedom and equality as promoted by liberalism and socialism were conceived as universal values for all human beings regardless of gender, age, race, religion, and nationality. Historically, though, the efforts made to obtain them always occurred within the institutional framework of nation- states. The two world wars of the first half of the 20th century demonstrated the invalidity of both liberalist cosmopolitanism and socialist internationalism when these are conceived within states pursuing their own interests, in a logic of power that cannot get out of the logic of Carl Schmitt's (1996 [1932]) friend–enemy contraposition. After the end of the Second World War II, the Cold War between the US and the Soviet Union created a bipolar order based on the terror of the possibility of atomic war. Taken together, the rupture of the ties between Eastern European states and the Soviet Union, the loosening of the Atlantic Alliance, the strengthening of the European Union, China's rise to great-power status, and the entry into the G20 of India and Brazil, as well as Japan, Saudi Arabia, Australia, Argentina, South Korea, and South Africa, all these transformations did not create a 'new' world order. With Russia's invasion of Ukraine, war has returned to European soil, and this is an ominous sign of the inability to form a united front and face the challenges produced by the crisis, as well as by the inequalities within each continent and state. This carries the risk of fuelling distrust among, and creating obstacles for, those who intend to look beyond the current circumstances.

International bodies have not failed to respond, but their reaction has been blatantly inadequate; once again, only the military powers ultimately decide on peace and war, and violence is legitimized by the us–them opposition. According to its charter, the United Nations organization cannot make decisions unless the five powers that enjoy the right of veto (the US, Russia, China, France and the UK) agree, and even when a resolution is reached, it lacks the tools to force states to implement it. The most evident case is the climate agreement reached in Paris in 2015, to limit global warming to no more than 1.5°C compared to the pre-industrial era; this is a strictly formal commitment if it does not specify who has to do what and when. It is clear that we cannot rely on the goodwill of states alone if we wish to address climate warming. Rather, we must make the energy transition a reality and abandon fossil fuels (coal and oil in the first instance, followed by gas and methane), replacing these with renewable energy sources: sun, air, and water. All this affects important geopolitical interests that determine the relations between producing and consuming countries, not to mention the interests of entire industrial sectors that have been responsible for the developments of the last century (the automobile industry, to name just one example). The required changes are truly impressive and – depending on a nation's position in social and geographical space – may affect lifestyles, ways of living, agricultural practices, animal husbandry, food habits, and short- to long-distance mobility. No aspect of life remains unaffected by the energy we produce and consume.

In the history of human societies, science and technology have been driven by three underlying trends: war, profit, and health. War spurred clever minds to produce ever- more powerful and refined tools to kill external enemies. Profit has driven the invention and production of increasingly sophisticated goods to meet real or imagined needs, but it has also led to the reduction of jobs and labour efforts. Health has pushed scientists and the healthcare industry to seek ways of reducing human suffering, guaranteeing healthy and possibly long lives, and freeing women from the obligation to devote their lives almost entirely to reproduction. It is to be hoped that the threat of the environmental crisis will induce science to change course, at least to some extent, and give priority to the survival of the species and the improvement of the quality of civilized life by fostering solidarity and directing development towards sustainability and the protection of the animal and plant environment. It is difficult to anticipate if sustainable development will fuel or restrain growth, and whether degrowth will be successful or not. Furthermore, it is very likely that, alongside the current growth in gross domestic product (GDP), other concepts and measurement tools will take into account economic dimensions that do not pass through the market and are not expressed in monetary terms. However, we can imagine future situations in which human beings spend less time standing in a traffic jam, working in a factory or office, and keeping themselves busy with electronic games; instead, they will devote their time to writing and reading poetry, playing an instrument or listening to a band, singing in a choir, practising a sport, performing on a theatre stage or watching a Shakespearean tragedy, as well as to helping a disabled neighbour or an elderly person who is no longer fully self-sufficient, or an immigrant or a refugee who has fled their country to escape persecution. It is not unrealistic to assume that networks of solidarity can be expanded and networks of relationships that reduce the isolation of the restricted private sphere can be built, perhaps through the very use of social networks. After all, it is only a matter of reknitting short-distance as well as long-distance community relationships, without demonizing the potential of new technologies.

The situation will change from country to country, and from culture to culture, depending on regimes and political systems that must nevertheless try to coexist while respecting each other's diversity. The decades ahead, which, as we have seen, will prove decisive in responding to the environmental crisis, will see the return of regressive and nostalgic tendencies of nationalisms that view globalization as a process that erases differences, levelling and homogenizing everything. Yet, we must hope and commit ourselves to ensure that the tendencies aiming at the governance of globalization will prevail, not only respecting but also valuing diversity at all levels, without compromising the effectiveness of common guidelines and policies.

All this will require a great deal of institution building, on the one hand, and a very high level of international cooperation, on the other – indeed, a world government capable of establishing and enforcing common rules. In sum, the current situation calls for a level of government at the planetary scale and the affirmation of an idea of global citizenship that coexists and is compatible with increasing levels of government and citizenship: local, regional, national, continental, and global. To put it differently, we must develop an idea of globalization as a process that brings together what was once distant and therefore requires the formation of a new culture of respect for diversity. In the past, what was far away could be ignored because it was inaccessible. Nowadays, the possibility of accessing what is different enables the recognition of otherness and the value of respect. In this way, if it abstains from building walls to recreate isolation and distance, the West can recognize and overcome the violence inflicted on peoples and cultures that have suffered the forms of domination that make up Western colonial history.

The idea of a unified world and global citizenship has already emerged throughout history. I am obviously referring to Immanuel Kant (and, by extension, the Age of Enlightenment), with his concept of perpetual peace, though also to currents of 19th-century liberal and socialist thought and, more recently, pacifist movements mobilized against the risk of atomic war, represented by the figures of Albert Einstein and Bertrand Russell. From 1863 – when Henri Dunant launched the first International Red Cross Conference – until the war in Ukraine, there has been an uninterrupted succession of wars and an equally incessant formation of pacifist movements. The memory of these wars has served not only to celebrate victories and commemorate the fallen but also to strengthen the desire for peace. The recent development of movements across the world, involving both the young and the old, demonstrates that their message (peace, environmental justice, the defence of biodiversity and civil and animal rights) has not fallen on deaf ears and that the conditions are in place for them to spread and grow. As Martha Nussbaum (1997) wrote back in 1997, it is a question of building new temporal horizons, starting from the teaching of the classics of Greek philosophy, which already nurtured the idea of a single humanity.

It is impossible to foresee what will prevail in the end – oblivion or memory – and whether the future will be short and conditioned by the present, or long and promising. We are, however, confident that the outcome is not deterministically predictable and that it is, therefore, worth striving for the construction of global citizenship.

References

Abrams, P. (1982) *Historical Sociology*, Ithaca, NY: Cornell University Press.

Adam, B. (1990) *Time and Social Theory*, Cambridge: Polity Press.

Adam, B. (1995) *Timewatch: The Social Analysis of Time*, Cambridge: Polity Press.

Adam, B. (1998) *Timescapes of Modernity: The Environment and Invisible Hazards*, London and New York, NY: Routledge.

Adam, B. (2004) *Time*, London: Polity Press.

Adam, B. and Groves, C. (2007) *Future Matters: Action, Knowledge, Ethics*, Leiden and Boston, MA: Brill.

Adorno, T.W. (1986 [1959]) 'The Meaning of Working through the Past', in G.H. Hartman (ed) *Bitburg in Moral and Political Perspective*, Bloomington, IN: Indiana University Press, pp 114–129.

Affuso, O. (2010) *Il Magazine della Memoria: I Media e il Ricordo degli Avvenimenti Pubblici*, Roma: Carocci.

Agamben, G. (2007 [1978]) *Infancy and History. On the Destruction of Experience*, London: Verso.

Alexander, J.C., Eyerman, R., Giesen, B., Smelser, N.J. and Sztompka, P. (2004) *Cultural Trauma and Collective Identity*, Oakland, CA: University of California Press.

Andersson, J. (2018) *The Future of The World: Futurology, Futurists, and the Struggle for the Post-Cold War Imagination*, Oxford: Oxford University Press.

Arendt, H. (1961) *Between Past and Future: Six Exercises in Political Thought*, New York, NY: The Viking Press.

Ariès, P. (1962) *Centuries of Childhood: A Social History of Family Life*, New York, NY: Penguin Books.

Assmann, A. (1998) *Der europäische Traum: Vier Lehren aus der Geschichte*, München: C.H. Beck.

Assmann, A. (2020) *Is Time Out of Joint? On the Rise and Fall of the Modern Regime*, Ithaca, NY: Cornell University Press.

Assmann, J. (2011 [1992]) *Cultural Memory and Early Civilizations*, Cambridge: Cambridge University Press.

Atia, N. and Davies, J. (2010) 'Nostalgia and the Shapes of History', *Memory Studies*, 3(3): 181–186.

Baudelaire, C. (2010 [1863]) *The Painter of Modern Life and Other Essays*, London: Penguin Books.

Bauman, Z. (1991) *Modernity and the Holocaust*, Cambridge: Polity Press.

Bauman, Z. (2017) *Retrotopia*, Cambridge: Polity Press.

Bellocchio, M. (dir) (2021) *Marx può aspettare*, Italy.

Benasayag, M. and Schmit, G. (2007) *Les Passions Tristes: Souffrance Psychique et Crise Sociale*, Paris: La Découverte.

Benjamin, W. (1968 [1940]) 'Theses on the Philosophy of History', in H. Arendt and H. Zohn (eds) *Illuminations*, New York, NY: Harcourt Brace Jovanovich, pp 253–264.

Benjamin, W. (2002 [1936]) 'The Storyteller: Observations on the Works of Nikolai Leskov', in H. Eiland and M.W. Jennings (eds) *Walter Benjamin: Selected Writings*, Vol. III, Cambridge, MA: Harvard University Press, pp 361–378.

Benjamin, W. (2003 [1940]) 'On Some Motifs in Baudelaire', in H. Eiland and M.W. Jennings (eds) *Walter Benjamin. Selected Writings*, Vol. IV, Cambridge, MA: Harvard University Press, pp 313–355.

Benjamin, W. (2005 [1929]) 'Surrealism. The Last Snapshot of the European Intelligentsia', in H. Eiland and M.W. Jennings (eds) *Walter Benjamin: Selected Writings*, Vol. II(1), Cambridge, MA: Harvard University Press, pp 207–221.

Bergmann, W. (1981) *Die Zeitstrukturen sozialer Systeme*, Berlin: Duncker & Humbolt.

Bergson, H. (1988 [1986]) *Matter and Memory*, New York, NY: Zone Books.

Berman, M. (1982) *All That Is Solid Melts into Air: The Experience of Modernity*, New York, NY: Penguin Books.

Berry, H., Bowen, K.J. and Kjellstrom, T. (2010) 'Climate Change and Mental Health', *International Journal of Public Health*, 55(2): 123–132.

Bloch, E. (1986 [1947]) *The Principle of Hope*, Cambridge, MA: MIT Press.

Block, L.F. (2018) *Capitalism: The Future of an Illusion*, Oakland, CA: University of California Press.

Blumenberg, H. (1986) *Lebenszeit und Weltzeit*, Frankfurt am Main: Suhrkamp.

Boccioni, U., Carrà, C., Russolo, L., Severini, G. and Balla, G. (1910) *Futurist Painting: Technical Manifesto*, Milano: Governing Group of the Futurist Movement.

Bourdieu, P. (1998) *Contre-Feux: Propos pour Servir à la Résistance Contre L'Invasion Néo-Libérale*, Paris: Liber-Raisons d'Agir.

Boym, S. (2001) *The Future of Nostalgia*, New York, NY: Basic Books.

Braudel, F. (1995) *A History of Civilizations*, New York, NY: Penguin Books.

Braun, E. (2004) 'Vulgarians at the Gate', in L. Mattioli Rossi (ed) *Boccioni's Materia: A Futurist Masterpiece and the Avant-Guarde in Milan and Paris*, New York, NY: Guggenheim, pp 1–21.

Brighenti, A.M. (2015) *Visibility in Social Theory and Social Research*, London, New York, NY and Shangai: Palgrave Macmillan.

Brockmeier, J. (2000) 'Autobiographical Time', *Narrative Inquiry*, 10(1): 51–73.

Bronfenbrenner, U. (1979) *The Ecology of Human Development: Experiments by Nature and Design*, Cambridge, MA: Harvard University Press.

Bryson, V. (2007) *Gender and the Politics of Time: Feminist Theory and Contemporary Debates*, Bristol: Bristol University Press.

Bury, J.B. (2023 [1920]) *The Idea of Progress: An Inquiry into Its Origin and Growth*, New York, NY: Aesterna Publishing.

Cassano, F. (2012) 'Thinking the Frontier', in F. Cassano, N. Bouchard and V. Ferme (eds) *Southern Thought and Other Essays on the Mediterranean*, New York, NY: Fordham University Press, pp 41–51.

Castells, M. (2000) *The Rise of the Network Society*, Hoboken, NJ: Blackwell.

Cavalli, A. (2013) 'The Memory of Fascism and of the Anti-Fascist Resistance among Italian Youth', *European Review*, 21(4): 501–506.

Cavalli, A. (2020) 'Generational Discontinuities and the Memory of Traumatic Events: The Case of Eastern Europe with a Special Focus on Germany', *European Review*, 28(6): 869–879.

Cerutti, F. (2007) *Global Challenges for the Leviathan: A Political Philosophy of Nuclear Weapons and Global Warming*, Lanham, MD: Lexington Books.

Chakrabarty, D. (2021) *The Climate of History in a Planetary Age*, Chicago, IL: Chicago University Press.

Chesnaux, J. (1996) *Habiter le Temps: Présent, Passé, Futur: Esquisse d'un Dialogue Politique*, Paris: Bayard Éditions.

Connerton, P. (2009) *How Modernity Forgets*, Cambridge: Cambridge University Press.

Conrad, S. (2018a) 'A Cultural History of Global Transformations', in S. Conrad and J. Osterhammel (eds) *An Emerging Modern World 1750–1870*, Cambridge: Belknap Press of Harvard University Press, pp 411–659.

Conrad, S. (2018b) '"Nothing Is the Way It Should Be": Global Transformations of the Time Regime in the Nineteenth Century', *Modern Intellectual History*, 15(3): 821–848.

Cook, J. (2018) *Imagined Futures: Hope, Risk and Uncertainty*, London, New York, NY and Shanghai: Palgrave Macmillan.

Crafts, N. and Toniolo, G. (eds) (1996) *Economic Growth in Europe since 1945*, Cambridge: Cambridge University Press.

Cuzzocrea, V. and Mandich, G. (2015) 'Students' Narratives of the Future: Imagined Mobilities as Forms of Youth Agency?', *Journal of Youth Studies*, 19(4): 552–567.

Cwerner, S.B. (2000) 'The Chronopolitan Ideal: Time, Belonging and Globalization', *Time & Society*, 9(2/3): 331–345.

Dechezleprêtre, A., Fabre, A., Kruse, T., Planterose, B., Sanchez Chico, A. and Stantcheva, S. (2022) 'Fighting Climate Change: International Attitudes toward Climate Policies', OECD Economics Department Working Papers, 1714.

Deeker, W. (2022) 'The COVID Generation: The Effects of the Pandemic on Youth's Mental Health', *Horizon: The EU Research & Innovation Magazine*, 20 January 2022. Available at: https://ec.europa.eu/research-and-innovation/en/horizon-magazine/covid-generation-effects-pandemic-youth-mental-health (accessed 6 April 2023).

Della Porta, D. and Diani, M. (2020) *Social Movements: An Introduction*, Chichester and Hoboken, NJ: Wiley-Blackwell.

Demetrio, D. (1994) *Raccontarsi: L'Autobiografia come Cura di Sé*, Milano: Cortina.

Di Chio, S. (2015) *Tempo Irreale: Il Restringimento dell'Orizzonte Temporale della Tarda Modernità*, Napoli: Liguori.

Dickens, C. (1993 [1861]) *Great Expectations*, Oxford: Clarendon Press.

Eco, U. (2000) *Apocalypse Postponed*, Bloomington, IN: Indiana University Press.

Eisenstadt, S.N. (2000) 'Multiple Modernities', *Daedalus*, 129: 1–29.

Eliade, M. (1959) *The Sacred and the Profane: The Nature of Religion*, New York, NY: Harcourt Brace Jovanovich.

Elias, N. (1994) *The Civilizing Process*, Oxford: Blackwell.

Elias, N. (2007 [1985]) *An Essay on Time*, Dublin: University College Dublin Press.

Fabian, J. (1983) *Time and the Other: How Anthropology Makes Its Object*, New York, NY: Columbia University Press.

Felice, E. (2022) *La Conquista dei Diritti: Un'Idea della Storia*, Bologna: Il Mulino.

Felski, R. (2000) *Doing Time: Feminist Theory and Postmodern Culture*, New York, NY and London: New York University Press.

Flaherty, M.G. (2013) 'Age and Agency: Time Work across the Life Course', *Time & Society*, 22(2): 237–253.

Flaherty, M.J. (2020) 'The Lathe of Time: Some Principles of Temporal Agency', in M.J. Flaherty, L. Meinert, and A.L. Dalsgård (eds) (2020) *Time Work: Studies of Temporal Agency*, New York, NY and Oxford: Berghahn Books, pp 13–28.

Flaherty, M.J., Meinert, L. and Dalsgård, A.L. (eds) (2020) *Time Work: Studies of Temporal Agency*, New York, NY and Oxford: Berghahn Books.

Gadamer, H.G. (2013 [1960]) *Truth and Method*, London: Bloomsbury Academic.

Gidley, M.J. (2017) *The Future: A Very Short Introduction*, Oxford: Oxford University Press.

Gilroy, P. (2005) *Postcolonial Melancholia*, New York, NY: Columbia University Press.

Golini, A. and Rosina, A. (eds) (2011) *Il Secolo degli Anziani: Come Cambierà l'Italia*, Bologna: Il Mulino.

Gospodinov, G. (2022) *Time Shelter*, New York, NY: Silverlight.

Guéguen, L. and Laurent, J. (2022) *La Perspective du Possible: Comment Penser ce qui Peut Nous Arriver, et ce que Nous Pouvons Faire*, Paris: Éditions La Découverte.

Habermas, J. (1986) 'Eine Art Schadensabwicklung', *Die Zeit*, 11 July.

Halbwachs, M. (1925) *Les Cadres Sociaux de la Mémoire*, Paris: Albin Michel.

Halbwachs, M. (1997 [1950]) *La Mémoire Collective*, édition critique établie par Gérard Namer, Paris: Albin Michel.

Halbwachs, M. (2008 [1941]) *La Topographie Légendaire des Évangiles en Terre Sainte*, Paris: P.U.F.

Hartog, F. (2015) *Regimes of Historicity: Presentism and Experiences of Time*, New York, NY: Columbia University Press.

Hartog, F. (2022) *Chronos: The West Confronts Time*, New York, NY: Columbia University Press.

Heberle, R. (1951) *Social Movements: An Introduction to Political Sociology*, New York, NY: Appleton-Century-Crofts.

Husserl, E. (1964 [1928]) *The Phenomenology of Internal Time-Consciousness*, Bloomington, IN: Indiana University Press.

Inglis, D. (2016) 'Globalization and/of Memory: On the Complexification and Contestation of Memory Cultures and Practices', in A.L. Tota and T. Hagen (eds) *Routledge International Handbook of Memory Studies*, London and New York, NY: Routledge, pp 143–157.

Jackson, T. (2021) *Post Growth: Life after Capitalism*, Cambridge: Polity Press.

Jameson, F. (2005) *Archaeologies of the Future*, London: Verso.

Jedlowski, P. (1986) *Il tempo dell'esperienza: Studi sul Concetto di Vita Quotidiana*, Milano: Franco Angeli.

Jedlowski, P. (2001) 'Memory and Sociology: Themes and Issues', *Time & Society*, 10(1): 29–44.

Jedlowski, P. (2016) 'Memories of the Future', in A.L. Tota and T. Hagen (eds) *Routledge International Handbook of Memory Studies*, London and New York, NY: Routledge, pp 121–130.

Jedlowski, P. and Pellegrino, V. (2020) 'Future as Horizon of Expectations', in J. Andersson and S. Kemp (eds) *Oxford Twenty-First Century Approaches to Literature Futures*, Oxford: Oxford University Press, pp 148–160.

Joas, H. (1996) *The Creativity of Action*, Chicago, IL: The Chicago University Press.

Jonas, H. (1984) *The Imperative of Responsibility: In Search of an Ethics for the Technological Age*, Chicago, IL: Chicago University Press.

Kaldor, M. (2003) *Global Civil Society: An Answer to War*, Cambridge: Polity Press.

Kandel, E.R. (2006) *In Search of Memory: The Emergence of a New Science of Mind*, New York, NY: W.W. Norton Company.

Kern, S. (1983) *The Culture of Time and Space 1880–1918*, Cambridge, MA: Harvard University Press.

Koselleck, R. (1985), *Futures Past: On the Semantics of Historical Time*, Cambridge, MA: MIT Press.

Koselleck, R. (2006) *Begriffsgeschichten*, Frankfurt am Main: Suhrkamp Verlag.

Koselleck, R. (2018) *Sediments of Time: On Possible History*, Stanford, CA: Stanford University Press.

LaCapra, D. (1994) *Representing the Holocaust: History, Theory, Trauma*, Ithaca, NY: Cornell University Press.

Lasch, C. (1979) *The Culture of Narcissism*, New York, NY: W.W. Norton Company.

Latouche, S. (2010 [2007]) *Farewell to Growth*, Cambridge: Polity Press.

Leccardi, C. (1996) 'Rethinking Social Time: Feminist Perspectives', *Time & Society*, 5(2): 169–186.

Leccardi, C. (2012) 'Young People's Representations of the Future and the Acceleration of Time: A Generational Approach', *Diskurs Kindheits und Jugendforschung*, 7(1): 59–73.

Leccardi, C. (2017) 'The Recession, Young People, and Their Relationship with the Future', in I. Schoon and J. Bynner (eds) *Young People's Development and the Great Recession: Uncertain Transitions and Precarious Futures*, Cambridge: Cambridge University Press, pp 348–371.

Leccardi, C. (2021) 'Redefining the Link between Structure and Agency: The Place of Time', in M. Nico and A. Caetano (eds) *Structure and Agency in Young People's Lives Theory, Methods and Agendas*, London: Routledge, pp 82–97.

Leitner, H. (1982) *Lebenslauf und Identität. Die kulturelle Konstruktion von Zeit in der Biographie*, Frankfurt am Main: Suhrkamp.

Lejeune, P. (1975) *Le Pacte Autobiographique*, Paris: Seuil.

Lévi-Strauss, C. (2020 [1962]) *Wild Thought*, Chicago, IL: The University of Chicago Press.

Levitas, R. (2013) *Utopia as Method: The Imaginary Reconstruction of Society*, London: Palgrave Macmillan.

Livi-Bacci, M. (1997) *A Concise History of World Population*, Cambridge: Blackwell.

Löckenhoff, C.E. and Rutt, J.L. (2015) 'Age Differences in Time Perception and Their Implications for Decision Making across the Life Span', in T.M. Hess, J. Strough and C.E. Löckenhoff (eds) *Aging and Decision Making: Empirical and Applied Perspectives*, London: Academic Press and Elsevier, pp 213–233.

Lowenthal, D. (2015) *The Past is a Foreign Country – Revisited*, Cambridge: Cambridge University Press.

Lübbe, H. (2009) 'The Contraction of the Present', in H. Rosa and W.E. Scheuerman (eds) *High-Speed Society: Social Acceleration, Power, and Modernity*, University Park, PA: Penn State University Press, pp 159–178.

Lucas, G. (dir) (1973) *American Graffiti*, USA.

Luckmann, T. (1993) 'Remarks on Personal Identity: Inner, Social and Historical Time', in A. Jacobson-Wigging (ed) *Identity: Personal and Socio-cultural: A Symposium*, Uppsala: Almqvist & Wiksell, pp 67–91.

Luhmann, N. (1976) 'The Future Cannot Begin: Temporal Structures in Modern Societies', *Social Research*, 43(1): 130–152.

Mandich, G. (ed) (2010) *Culture quotidiane*, Roma: Carocci.

Mannheim, K. (1952 [1928]) 'The Problem of Generations', in P. Kecskemeti (ed) *Essays on the Sociology of Knowledge*, London: Routledge and Kegan Paul, pp 276–320.

Marchesoni, S. (2016) *Walter Benjamins Konzept des Eingedenkens*, Berlin: Kadmos.

Martuccelli, D. (2017) *La condition sociale moderne: L'avenir d'une inquiétude*, Paris: Gallimard.

Marx, K. (1993 [1857–58]) *Grundrisse: Foundations of the Critique of Political Economy*, London: Penguin Classics.

Mead, G.H. (1954 [1932]) *The Philosophy of the Present*, Chicago, IL: Open Court Publishing Company.

Meadows, D.H., Meadows, D.L., Randers, J. and Behrens, W. (1972) *The Limits to Growth*, New York, NY: Universe Books.

Melucci, A. (1989) *Nomads of the Present: Social Movements and Individual Needs in Contemporary Society*, Philadelphia, PA: Temple University Press.

Melucci, A. (1996) *Challenging Codes: Collective Action in the Information Age*, Cambridge: Cambridge University Press.

Merck, C., N'Topcu, M. and Hirst, W. (2016) 'Collective Mental Time Travel: Creating a Shared Future through Our Shared Past', *Memory Studies*, 9(3): 284–294.

Morag, R. (2013) *Waltzing with Bashir. Perpetrator Trauma and Cinema*, London: I.B. Tauris & Co.

Namer, G. (1987) *Mémoire et Societé*, Paris: Klincksieck.

Namer, G. (1997) 'Postface', in M. Halbwachs (ed) *La Mémoire Collective*, édition critique établie par Gérard Namer, Paris: Albin Michel, pp 239–295.

Namer, G. (2000) *Halbwachs et la Mémoire Sociale*, Paris: L'Harmattan.

Nisbet, R. (2017 [1980]) *History of the Idea of Progress*, Abingdon and New York, NY: Routledge.

Nolan, C. (dir) (2000) *Memento*, USA.

Nowotny, H. (1994) *Time: The Modern and Postmodern Experience*, Cambridge: Polity Press.

Nowotny, H. (2021) *In AI We Trust. Power, Illusion and Control of Predicting Algorithms,* Cambridge: Polity Press.

Nussbaum, M.C. (1997) *Cultivating Humanity: A Classical Defense of Reform in Liberal Education*, Cambridge, MA: Harvard University Press.

Olick, J.K., Vinitzky Seroussi, V. and Levy, D. (eds) (2011) *The Collective Memory Reader*, Oxford: Oxford University Press.

Orwell, G. (1949) *1984*, London: Penguin Books.

Pellizzoni, L., Leonardi, E. and Asara V. (eds) (2022) *Handbook of Critical Environmental Politics*, Cheltenham: Edward Elgar Publishing.

Pleyers, G. (2020) 'The Pandemic Is a Battlefield: Social Movements in the COVID-19 Lockdown', *Journal of Civil Society*, 16(4): 295–312.

Pomian, K. (1980) 'La Crise de l'Avenir', *Le Debat*, 7: 5–17.

Pomian, K. (1984) *L'Ordre du Temps*, Paris: Gallimard.

Pulcini, E. (2013) *Care of the World: Fear, Responsibility and Justice in the Global Age*, Dordrecht: Springer.

Rainey, L., Poggi, C. and Wittman, L. (1999) *Futurism: An Anthology*, New Haven, CT and London: Yale University Press.

Ricoeur, P. (1994) 'Le Concept de Responsabilité: Essai d'Analyse Sémantique', *Esprit*, 206(11): 28–48.

Ricoeur, P. (2004) *Memory, History, Forgetting*, Chicago, IL: The University of Chicago Press.

Ricoeur, P., Larre, C., Pannikar, R., Kagame, A., Lloyd, G.E.R., Neher, A. et al (1975) *Les Cultures et Les Temps*, Paris: Payot.

Rosa, H. (2003) 'Social Acceleration: Ethical and Political Consequences of a Desynchronized High-Speed Society', *Constellations*, 10(1): 3–33.

Rosa, H. (2010) *Alienation and Acceleration: Towards a Critical Theory of Late-modern Temporality*, Malmö and Aarhus: NSU Press.

Rosa, H. (2013) *Social Acceleration: A New Theory of Modernity*, New York, NY: Columbia University Press.

Rosa, H. and Scheuerman, W.E. (eds) (2009) *High-Speed Society: Social Acceleration, Power, and Modernity*, University Park, PA: Penn State University Press.

Rosenthal, G. (1997) *The Holocaust in Three Generations: Families of Victims and Perpetrators of the Nazi-Regime*, London: Cassell.

Schacter, D.L. and Welker, M. (2016) 'Memory and Connection: Remembering the Past and Imagining the Future in Individuals, Groups, and Cultures', *Memory Studies*, 9(3): 241–244.

Schiavone, A. (2022) *What is Progress*, New York, NY: Europa Editions.

Schizzerotto, A., Trivellato, U. and Sartor, N. (eds) (2011) *Generazioni Disuguali: Le Condizioni di Vita dei Giovani di Ieri e di Oggi*, Bologna: Il Mulino.

Schleicher, A. (2018) *World Class: How to Build a 21st-Century School System*, Paris: OECD.
Schmitt, C. (1996 [1932]) *The Concept of the Political*, Chicago, IL: The University of Chicago Press.
Schutz, A. and Luckmann, T. (1973) *The Structures of the Life-World*, Vol. I, Evanston, IL: Northwestern University Press.
Snow, C.P. (1959) *The Two Cultures and the Scientific Revolution*, Cambridge: Cambridge University Press.
Spencer, M.E. (1982) 'Social Science and the Consciousness of the Future', *Theory and Society*, 11(5): 683–712.
Spengler, O. (1962 [1918]) *The Decline of the West*, New York, NY: Alfred A. Knopf.
Szondi, P. (1978 [1961]) 'Hope in the Past: On Walter Benjamin', *Critical Inquiry*, 4(3): 491–506.
Tabboni, S. (2001) 'The Idea of Social Time in Norbert Elias', *Time & Society*, 10(1): 5–27.
Taguieff, P.A. (2000) *L'Effacement de l'Avenir*, Paris: Galilée.
Taguieff, P.A. (2004) *Le Sens du Progrès: Un Approche Historique et Philosophique*, Paris: Flammarion Éditions.
Tarrow, S. (1989) *Struggle, Politics and Reform: Collective Action, Social Movements and Cycles of Protest*, Ithaca, NY: Cornell University Press.
Tomelleri, S. (2015) *Ressentiment: Reflections on Mimetic Desire and Society*, East Lansing, MI: Michigan State University.
Torres, F. (2022) *Temporal Regimes: Materiality, Politics, Technology*, New York, NY: Routledge.
Torres, F. and Gros, A. (2022) 'Slowing Down Society? Theoretical Reflections on Social Deceleration in Pandemic Times (and Beyond)', *KronoScope*, 22(1): 3–29.
Torres, F. and Rosa, H. (2021) 'Acceleration Theory, Temporal Regimes, and Politics Today: An Interview with Hartmut Rosa', *Res Publica*, 24(3): 519–523.
Tota, A.L. and Hagen, T. (eds) (2016) *Routledge International Handbook of Memory Studies*, London and New York, NY: Routledge.
Traverso, E. (2016) *Left-Wing Melancholia: Marxism, History and Memory*, New York, NY: Columbia University Press.

Turner, V. (1982) *From Ritual to Theatre: The Human Seriousness of Play*, New York, NY: Performing Arts Journal Publications.

Vignoli, D., Minello, A., Bazzani, G., Matera, C. and Rapallini, C. (2022) 'Narratives of the Future Affect Fertility: Evidence from a Laboratory Experiment', *European Journal of Population*, 38: 93–124.

Virilio, P. (2000) *Polar Inertia*, London: Sage.

Wagner, P. (2016) *Progress: A Reconstruction*, Cambridge: Polity Press.

Weber, M. (2012) *Max Weber: Collected Methodological Writings* (eds H.H. Bruun and S. Whimster), London: Routledge.

Weinrich, H. (2004) *Lethe: The Art and Critique of Forgetting*, Ithaca, NY: Cornell University Press.

Wilson, S. and Jaffé, D. (eds) (2017) *Memories of the Future: On Countervision*, Oxford and New York, NY: Peter Lang.

Woodman, D. and Wyn, J. (2014) *Youth and Generation: Rethinking Change and Inequality in the Lives of Young People*, London: Sage.

Wray, B. (2022) *Generation Dread: Finding Purpose in an Age of Climate Crisis*, Toronto: Alfred A. Knopf Canada.

Wyn, J., Cahill, H., Woodman, D., Cuervo, H., Leccardi, C. and Chesters, J. (eds) (2020) *Youth and the New Adulthood: Generations of Change*, Singapore: Springer.

Index

D

Printed in the USA
CPSIA information can be obtained
at www.ICGtesting.com
JSHW051720061123
51546JS00005B/25

9 781529 213973